VALUE

How to talk about what you do
so people want to buy it

Also by Robyn Haydon:

The Shredder Test: A step-by-step guide to writing winning proposals

Winning Again: A retention game plan for your most important contracts and customers

VALUE

How to talk about what you do
so people want to buy it

ROBYN HAYDON

Durban Professionals Press

First published 2016
Durban Professionals Press

Cover design by Dark Labs
Author photograph & diagrams by Stephanie Teh
Edited by Stephanie Teh
Typesetting by Sylvie Blair

Disclaimer

The material in this book is general comment only and neither purports nor intends to be specific advice related to any particular reader. It does not represent professional advice and should not be relied on as the basis for any decision or action on any matter that it covers. To the maximum extent permitted by law, the author and publisher disclaim all responsibility and liability to any person or entity, whether a purchaser or not, in respect to anything and of the consequences of anything done by any such person in reliance, whether in whole or in part, upon the whole or any part of the contents of this publication.

National Library of Australia Cataloguing-in-Publication entry

Creator: Haydon, Robyn, author.

Title: Value : how to talk about what you do so people want to

buy it / written by Robyn Haydon ;

edited by Stephanie Teh.

ISBN: 9781925457155 (paperback) eISBN: 9781925457162

Dewey Number: 658.812

Acknowledgements

Thank you to my early readers, Nadine Sanderson, Trudi Giouris, Stan Pappos and Jane Anderson, who provided invaluable feedback that shaped the final version of this book.

Thank you to Matt Church, who suggested that despite having already written two books on business development topics, perhaps I wasn't quite done yet. This book is the result.

And finally, to Steph and Zach, who I value more than anything else in the world – thank you for believing in me.

Contents

Foreword

WHY IS IT SO hard to win new business?

That's a good question – and this book is designed to help you answer it.

I am a business development consultant who specialises in helping people to win and retain customers through competitive bids, tenders and large-scale proposals.

The work I do involves working with teams to build an offer for a prospective customer completely from the ground up – every time – in response to what that customer needs, and will value.

Over the course of nearly two decades, I've helped people to win hundreds of millions of dollars worth of business in complex services industries, including:

1. Government-funded human services;

2. Large-scale enterprise services, like information technology, programmed maintenance, and logistics; and

3. Professional services such as engineering, project management, finance and law.

What really lights me up about the work I do is that I have the opportunity to help smart people find the connection between what they know and can do, and what makes commercial sense for customers to buy.

But this work is by no means easy.

There's no doubt that it is a buyer's market now. Competitive tenders are the norm for contracts of any size and value. And in every market, with information so easy to come by, buyers are often two-thirds or more through their decision making process by the time they get to us. By then we've lost the power to influence them.

This has some unintended knock-on effects that, for the most part, aren't being talked about very much – yet.

The move to compulsory competitive tendering has dampened the contribution of the best and brightest people within supplier organisations. This is a worrying trend.

The most common thing I hear, when talking to senior leaders inside these organisations about their business development challenges, is this:

> *My people avoid tenders like the plague – I'd love to find a way to get them enthusiastic, engaged, and actually wanting to work on them. Is this something you can help with?*

The answer is yes – and no.

- No, because the best and brightest people, for the most part, don't want to work on 'tenders'. They don't want to be dictated to by a customer who doesn't know as much as they do.

- Yes, because what really motivates smart people is the chance to use their brains to create things that have real impact and value for customers. That's something I am passionate about – and it's why I wrote this book.

I'm concerned about the implications of supplier disengagement, if it continues. Many of the wonderful people and organisations who do great work, which we all benefit from, may struggle to make the contribution we need them to make, and to realise their true potential.

This book is for people who work in services industries and in services-based professions.

If you're drawn to this kind of work, you probably want to use your expertise to help others, to do good work, and to make a difference. But in the real world, we must first convince people that they *need* our help; we have to convince them to buy from us. And this isn't always as easy as it should be.

Products are fairly straightforward to sell, because we can touch them, feel them, and understand through experiencing them how they work.

Services on the other hand, are not straightforward at all. Like a product, a service solves a problem, but the problem is often hard to see, and may be completely unknown to the person who is experiencing it.

As a result, people are often suspicious of buying services, because they don't understand them and are worried that they might never get the outcome that they were promised.

But these people – let's call them customers – have real problems that we can solve, and they need our help. It's our duty and responsibility to get out there and help them, but this means getting past our own fears and biases first.

Doing is easy. Selling can be hard.

Back in Renaissance Italy, artists were supported by wealthy patrons who admired their work. This system had benefits for both parties.

Artists received a living wage, access to luxury materials (such as gold and lapis lazuli) and commissions to produce art on a size and scale they could otherwise only dream of. Patrons used the art they produced as a means of expressing and enhancing their social status. Without this patronage system, we wouldn't have many of the works of brilliant artists like Leonardo da Vinci, Michelangelo or Raphael.

In service industries, we also need to find patrons – customers –who get what we do, and who see the mutual benefit in commissioning us to do it. This is essential if we are to have any chance of bringing our gifts into the world.

It's easy to accept the excuse that it is all about price and that customers don't want what we have anymore. That isn't really true. They may want it – and they probably need it – but like the rest of us, they are time-poor, risk-averse and battered by disruption and change. Consequently, we need to give them extremely compelling reasons to do things the way that we suggest.

VALUE will help you to look at what you do in an entirely new way; from the perspective of how it creates commercial value for customers, in a way that motivates them to buy.

It will help you to identify what you're really selling; to be very clear on the value it offers to the people who might want to buy it; and to speak confidently about it to someone who doesn't understand it nearly as well as you do.

This book is written in three parts.

- In the first part, Identity, we'll look at what we buy as consumers, and how it affects the way we see ourselves. We'll examine the reasons why buyers and sellers have ended up so far apart, when we actually want the same thing. We'll see how for sellers, the current buying environment can easily erode the joy of service and replace it with something far less pleasant...subservience and servitude.

- In the second part, Commoditisation, we'll examine the forces that are driving prices down and forcing us into boxes we don't want to fit into, and how we can swim out of the 'sea of same'.

- And in the third part, Value, we'll unpack the three drivers and six primary attributes that create commercial value for customers, and look at how you can build an offer that your prospects would be crazy to say no to.

If you have ever missed out on an opportunity that you really deserved to win, ever struggled to explain what you offer to people who just don't seem to understand, or if you've ever seen prospective customers stubbornly go down a path that you know is not right for them – then this book is for you.

I hope that this book will spark many useful ideas about how you can explain the commercial value of what you do in a way that helps customers decide to buy from you.

I also hope you'll want to refer back to it time and time again, when you get stuck, or when something isn't working, to help you figure out what to change.

Finally, I'd love to think that *Value* will help you to unlock your potential, and live your purpose, and to do that through the opportunity to serve others. Don't let your confidence, and the joy in what you do, get chipped away by years of responding to what other people say they want, or worse, by constantly having them say 'no' to you.

Ultimately, value is in the eye of the beholder, and it can be challenging to be both the actor and audience in your own play.

It is enormously helpful to have a sounding board when you're seeking to unpack and understand the true value in what you do.

Talk to your colleagues, talk to friends, and if you need help, please reach out to me.

It would be my privilege and pleasure to help you win the business you deserve to win, and to make the impact I know you can make.

ROBYN HAYDON

PART 1

Identity

We are all consumers, and what we buy affects the way we see ourselves. Here we'll examine the reasons why buyers and sellers have ended up so far apart, when we actually want the same thing. We'll also discover how our own attitudes towards customers can land us in unrewarding roles like servitude and subservience, and why rising above these roles is the first step towards our real goal – to be of service.

CHAPTER 1

We are what we buy

Like many other households in the 1970s, ours contained a set of encyclopedias that lined the bookshelves in the mission-brown family room. Our encyclopedia subscription also came with a bonus 'annual' volume that arrived each year.

As a child, I was a voracious reader who would even read the back of the cornflakes packet if there was nothing else available, so I really looked forward to these information-packed treats.

One year, the annual was about Dogs. After devouring that book with a passion, I can still recognise obscure dogs on the street just from what I can still recall from the drawings of the different breeds.

Another year, the annual was about Psychology. What I remember the most about that book was a section containing four photos of the same woman, shown from different viewpoints. From my recollection, these were:

1. As the camera sees her (pleasant and smiling, with a slightly hesitant expression),

2.   As she sees herself (vampy and knowing, with teased hair and a beauty spot),

3.   As her husband sees her (mousy and downcast, with drooping shoulders), and

4.   As her friends see her (loud and brash, but a bit dishevelled).

As a young person yet to hit puberty, this was my first introduction to the idea that there was more than one way to look at the world (mine).

And in my work, I have been fascinated ever since by the way that we reflect our identity in what, and who, we choose to buy.

"Who am I?"

It's a big question, and one that has occupied psychologists and sociologists for hundreds of years.

A more useful question, when it comes to buying and selling, is "How do I see myself, and who do I want to be?"

We all have an identity that we want to show to the world, and we confirm that identity through our actions. Therefore, what we buy, and who we buy it from, both affect the way we see ourselves.

Let's look at a few examples.

•   If you'd like to be seen as a good person, someone with integrity, you might be on the lookout for ways to 'do the right thing' – probably without even realising it. As a result, you might find that you end up buying ethical, environmentally or 'green' products and services over alternative options.

- If you'd like to be known as a generous person, someone who gives to others, you might find yourself sponsoring a child in a developing country, or contributing to (and sharing) online fundraising campaigns.

- If you'd like to be seen as a frugal person, who is good with money, you might enjoy sniffing out a bargain and sharing these good deals with your admiring friends and family.

- Or if you want to be seen as a productive person, who gets things done, you might like trying out and talking about gadgets that help you to do more in a day and to make the most of your time.

We all buy things, and we all play roles while we're doing it.

In going about your day-to-day purchases, you probably don't give a lot of thought or attention to this. However, identity shapes all of our buying decisions – both good and bad.

Have you ever bought something you thought was absolutely amazing and couldn't wait to tell your friends about it? When I ask people this question, their answers vary widely:

- One of my clients has a favourite pair of boxing shoes that she can't be without. When she can't find them before going to the gym, she will up-end her house to look for them.

- Another client mentioned that his son bought a pair of waterproof Bluetooth speakers for diving. Apparently these are the coolest things he's ever seen and he never stops talking about them.

- Yet another is a car enthusiast, who bought a Mercedes recently. He has a vivid recollection of the whole experience, from the barista in the store to the gift-wrapped vehicle to the after-sales courtesy and service.

Everyone has something that their life wouldn't be the same without. Even if you don't actually love this thing, you probably still rely on it. Some examples are your mobile phone, road bike or perhaps even your custom made car keys that can only be replaced via courier from Europe.

For me, it's an application on my phone called *rev.com*. In my line of work I write a lot of words. Using this transcription app has helped me to catch on my thoughts on the fly, have them transcribed into text, and has saved me many, many hours of work. I tell everyone I know about this app, particularly those who work in consulting businesses or in mobile professions like project management and engineering. (You're welcome).

What we value supports our identity, and makes us feel good about ourselves.

My client's boxing shoes fit her identity as a person who makes it a priority to exercise. The waterproof Bluetooth speakers make the teenage son a cool person who is up with the latest gadgets and can clue in his friends (the way I said that was probably not cool at all). The transcription app I use makes me highly productive, which is an identity I aspire to.

On the other hand, have you ever bought something that turned out to be a dud?

Bad products, services or investments are memorable for all the wrong reasons – because of all the pain they put us through.

- One of my clients told me about an investment property that she had purchased, but had to sell quickly during a market downturn. She lost tens of thousands of dollars on that transaction.

- Another client hired a guy to do some exterior work around his house. The man had been in jail before, but my client wanted to give him another chance. Unfortunately, he disappeared with the deposit and my client never saw him, or any work, again.

- My partner and I bough a timeshare while on holiday in Thailand more than a decade ago. Only when we got back home did we realise that it was going to take at least 10 hours on a plane to get to any of the gorgeous places we'd fallen in love with, and the local ones we could swap our 'weeks' for weren't worth the money. We couldn't get any cash back because of the way the scheme was set up.

While we might tell a lot of people about the things that we love and that have made us happy, we rarely mention the duds – even if these cautionary tales might stop other people from making a similar mistake.

That's because it hurts our identity to relate these stories. My partner and I don't tell a lot of people about the timeshare (although now I've told all of you), because it makes us look like chumps who were taken in by a slick sales pitch – which, of course, we were.

Identity is at the core of every buying decision. Because we all buy things, we can all get better at persuading others to buy. Mostly, this is called 'selling'.

Selling requires the ability to put yourself in another person's position, and to appeal to their identity – whether you're selling to consumers or to business buyers.

The *I Bought A Jeep* campaign is a good example of how identity affects purchase behaviour. This campaign, launched in 2012, has become part of the Australian cultural vernacular.

The advertising firm behind the campaign, Cummins&Partners, discovered that although Jeeps were very popular with the people who already drove them, the brand was struggling to reach new customers with its previous ad campaign slogan, *Don't Hold Back*.

Qualitative research with current Jeep customers showed that most of them had experienced an 'incredulous' reaction from family and friends when explaining they'd bought a Jeep ("you bought a WHAT?").

The big idea behind the new campaign was to dramatise this as 'incredulous approval'. Therefore, the reaction to saying "I bought a Jeep" became "You bought a Jeep!"

Jeep's brand values are freedom, authenticity, adventure and passion, and the ads tap into a customer's desire to live those values – not just buy a car.

This campaign won two Silver awards at the advertising industry's 2014 Australian Effie Awards. The agency's submission to the awards committee shows that the campaign had dramatically increased sales for the parent company, Fiat Chrysler, in a difficult car sales market. Since the start of the campaign, Jeep sales increased 156%, outgrowing the SUV category by 300% while also reducing media expenditure per unit by 45%.

Australia is now Jeep's second largest sales market outside the USA. Talking about the success of the campaign, Cummins&Partners' CEO Sean Cummins said:

> Our aim is to create enduring platforms for brands that inspire action. And this does both. In spades. What is exciting for us is that 'I bought a Jeep' has become so idiomatic to Australians. This is the stuff brands dream of. And it is a sensational platform that could go for years...the work we do is not for the industry, it is for consumers. And they are buying Jeeps!

Knowing what we know about how the ads play to the connection between Jeep's brand values and the values of the customer, we could also add to this by concluding:

"...because we found a way to appeal to the buyer's identity."

What you do is already awesome

We are often too close to what we do to get a true picture of its value and usefulness to others. This is because our relatively complex maps of what and how we do things result in a cognitive bias known in psychological circles as 'functional fixedness.'

Functional fixedness means that our thinking has evolved in a way that limits us to using an object (or an idea) only in the way that we are accustomed to using it.

In 1945, Gestalt psychologist Karl Duncker defined functional fixedness as being a "mental block against using an object in a new way that is required to solve a problem."

In his classic experiment, Duncker gave participants a candle, a box of thumbtacks, and a book of matches, and asked them to attach the candle to the wall so that it did not drip onto the table below. He found that people tried many unsuccessful ways to solve the problem – including attaching the candle directly to the wall with the tacks, or gluing it to the wall by melting it – but very few of them thought of the inside of the box of thumbtacks as a candle-holder, and tacking this to the wall instead. When he repeated the experiment, giving people a box that was now empty of thumbtacks, they were almost twice as likely to solve the problem.

The older we get, and the more experience we gain, the more likely we are to exhibit 'functional fixedness'.

Let's say you have a complex problem at work. To nut it out, you have a chat to your partner (who works in a field that is completely different to yours) while you are both making dinner.

After a few minutes of you talking about the problem, they say "Oh, so you mean it's about *XXX*?"

And of course it is. They are able to 'get it' because their map of the subject is different to yours (and also because they're not trying to verbally process it at the same time).

Tests have shown that children aged 5 years have no signs of functional fixedness, but by age 7 have acquired the tendency to treat the originally intended purpose of an object as special.

This might explain why you can tip a box of Lego on the floor of a kindergarten and the three and four-year-olds will just go for it, making the most weird and wonderful creations, whereas school-age children often prefer being given a Lego box containing the parts and instructions to make something tangible, like a car or plane.

As well as making it more challenging to think laterally to solve problems, there is another impact of functional fixedness – our inability to acknowledge what we do as valuable, and special.

Imagine you're having a beer with an old friend, who asks about what you're doing at work these days. You tell them a bit about the project you're working on, only to have them exclaim, "Oh my God, that's amazing!" To you, it might just seem like another day in the office. But to them, what you're doing is pretty remarkable.

As you read this book, I'd like you to hold onto the possibility that what you do is already awesome, and that all we need to do is find a way to explain it to others so that they get it – and want to buy it.

The widening gap between buyers and sellers

ONCE UPON A TIME, and not so very long ago, a group of smart people went to work solely to help other people – their customers.

Every day, they used their skills and expertise to solve health problems, to build bridges and buildings, invent new technologies, get people jobs, and make products that were better, safer and more effective. And everyone was happy.

One day, a different group of people came along – the procurement people. Their job was to buy things, including the services that the other smart people offered, and to do that in a way that was better, cheaper, and more efficient.

Because of that, things started to change for the smart people. They started to become known as 'suppliers'. There were new rules for how their customers could hire them. They started having to spend more and more of their time writing proposals, responding to tenders and negotiating prices and contracts. Sometimes, this forced them to agree to do things that they knew were not smart, or right, or necessary, and to give up doing things that were.

The smart people became very sad. The excitement of work started to dim a bit. Some were angry. Some were scared. Some lost their confidence. Many lost customers too. And all of them longed to go back to the good old days, when customers cared more about their skills and expertise, and they were just able to get on with the job of helping people.

Discouraged, many smart people stopped coming up with new ways to help their customers. "What's the point?" they thought. "Customers aren't interested any more – they will just tell us what they want instead."

Over time, some of these customers realised that in fact they hadn't been making the best decisions. Things took longer, cost more and didn't work as well as they did when the smart people were truly invested in helping them.

At the same time, some of the smart people started to see that their customers were exhausted by constant change and disruption, and that they were missing out on opportunities that would really make a difference. Those smart people resolved to help them in the only way they could – by changing the way they were going about the task of solving customer problems and creating customer value.

Sound like a fairy tale? It's happening right now in relationships between buyers and suppliers. If you want to see everyone live happily ever after, you have a chance to be a part of the solution.

The problem with selling services

When we want to be of service to others, it's exceptionally frustrating when some – including those who seem to be in the greatest need – are unwilling to let us do exactly that. Why does this happen, and what can we do about it?

I bet you've sat in many meetings where prospects have explained problems that you know you are exquisitely qualified to solve.

You've heard their aspirations and been able to see instantly how you can achieve them. Seen how the course of action they have mapped out in their heads will land them in a place that they really don't want to go. Felt the excitement of knowing you have a solution that can really help them.

The conversation goes well – they like you and you like them. It should be a total no-brainer that you'll do business together. Yet this is not always what happens. Why?

In the sales profession, in sales training programs within organisations, and in most books about sales, there's a lot of discussion about 'how' to sell.

And there's no doubt that methodology and process – knowing how to do something – is useful. Modern sales methodologies have helped an enormous number of people, including me. Sometimes, making a change to the way you do things can make a big difference to your results.

But even the best process in the world cannot help, if what you are selling is not what customers want to buy.

This is not a book about how; it's about what you are selling. When you're selling services, often it's the *what* and not the *how* that is the problem.

Almost every bestselling book written about sales and marketing talks about 'products'. The examples they give, and the methodologies they describe, relate to tangible things that people can see, hear, and handle.

Services are different.

When we think of services we tend to think first of professional services, like taxation or legal advice.

Actually, services are any input that a person, organisation, or community needs in order to achieve its goals.

Services are the building blocks of getting things done. They're part of making products; making buildings, bridges and rockets to Mars; and of making lives better in the community.

The team of engineers developing a sanitation system for a new urban village is delivering a service.

So are the clinicians helping people in the community who struggle with addiction, mental health issues and domestic abuse.

So are the IT specialists helping government to build a new medical records system, the project managers helping property developers to shave 20% off their construction costs, and the career coach helping a retrenched manager to build their confidence and get a new job.

Services are everywhere, and they are a large – and defining – part of the economies of educated, developed nations and of how we will create our future.

The growth of the service economy underpins the economic growth of a nation.

A study by the World Bank showed that in high-income countries, services represented 66% of GDP (gross domestic product), compared with only 35% in low-income countries.

The Australian Bureau of Statistics reports that the services industries here employ more than 8.6 million people, representing 76% of all employment. The largest employing service industry is Health care and social assistance, with average annual employment in 2010–11 of 1,291,800 people, accounting for 15% of total employment in the services sector. Other large employing industries are Retail trade (1,234,400 people), Education and training (866,900 people), and Professional, scientific and technical services (861,000 people).

That's a lot of people who work in services industries and who need help to sell what they do.

Yet services can be hard to understand and define, making them very difficult to sell.

As early as 1981, Prof. Valerie Zeithaml of Texas A&M University identified that professional services exist on the extreme intangibility end of the tangibility spectrum. "Their 'product' is the result of many years of specialised study and training, and clients have difficulty evaluating these products", she said.

In other words, because you can neither see, touch, smell, taste nor hear services, we may as well be selling fairy dust.

Because of this, there's a lot of mistrust of service providers by those who buy services.

Although they probably won't say it to your face, here's what they are thinking:

- *What does this really mean, anyway?*

- *How do I know you will do what you say you will?*

- *Will I actually get the team you're proposing?*

- *How does this fit with the other stuff I am working on?*

- *How do I know this will get results?*

- *Is this going to be hard for me to manage, or justify to my boss?*

- *Does it really cost that much?*

- *That doesn't look too hard...tell me again why I really need you, anyway?*

Complex services – like health and human services, large-scale enterprises services, and professional services – are, by definition, complex and time-consuming to execute.

That's why the customer needs us.

Unfortunately, this also makes them complex and time-consuming to explain, which means we feel under constant pressure to get straight into unpacking our methodology and implementation plan – what and how. This often comes at the expense of explaining the problem we're solving (why), which from the customer's perspective is the only reason why they would even consider buying from us.

According to Daniel Pink, author of *To Sell is Human*, the qualities of Attunement, Buoyancy and Clarity (A-B-C) are what's needed to be effective in today's world of sales, where buyers and sellers are evenly matched on information. This makes pretty good sense.

In terms of how we put these principles in practice, though, we actually want to think in terms of C-A-B:

1. **Clarity** means knowing what you are really selling, understanding the value it creates for a customer, and being able to articulate why they should buy it. Clarity comes from focusing squarely on value (why) rather than methodology (what and how). Clarity needs comes first, because without clarity nothing else really matters.

2. **Attunement** means being able to understand what buyers want. Most popular sales and marketing books are about attunement, because figuring out what buyers want is what most people associate with success. However, 'wants' are only part of the value puzzle, as we'll discover later. As an expert selling a complex service, and who wants to deliver great work as a result, attunement needs to go both ways – not only to what buyers want, but also to what they really need.

3. **Buoyancy** means being able to overcome rejection, so you can keep going until you get a result. Many selling skills

methodologies focus on buoyancy (resilience) because it is what veteran salespeople understand is the key to longevity. By selling value, though, we will experience less rejection, and thankfully also need to rely less on being able to rebound like a human punching bag.

Another reason to start with Clarity is that it's the only one of these three attributes where we can exert total control.

Attunement and Buoyancy both require that we develop strategies to respond to factors external to ourselves, which is much more challenging, and pretty much impossible when we don't have Clarity.

In this book, we're going to examine what you really do, the results that you're creating, and what is truly remarkable about your work.

That understanding – that clarity – is the key to winning the business you want, at the margins you want, and making the difference you alone can make.

Risky business

When I talk to people about a contract that is up for tender, or a project they'd like to do, or a piece of new business they would love to win, there are several things that they usually tell me.

The first is that this venture has their name written all over it; that they are the ideal people for the job. They've got the credentials, the methodology, the people, and the skills to get the job done.

Something else I hear a lot is that it's an 'ideal fit' for their vision, mission or strategic plan – or it just fits their image of where they'd like to go in future.

Another thing that people often say is that they would love to have the opportunity to do this kind of project or to work with that customer; that it would look great on their CV or would help them attract other, similar business.

Interestingly, the pragmatic arguments – that there is significant money to be made, or a chance to beat competitors – often come well behind, or aren't mentioned at all.

All of these aspirations have a common theme; that first and foremost, most of us want to do interesting work and to make a difference. We tend to approach a pitch with an 'opportunity' mindset.

On the other hand, when looking at the same contract, project or tender, prospective customers have a completely different set of thoughts going through their mind.

- *This is a really important project. It needs to go well.*

- *If it doesn't go well, it's my job or my reputation on the line.*

- *There's a whole bunch of things I want done, but I don't know if those things are really possible, and I don't know if I trust you to do them for me or not.*

- *I'd love to make an impact with this project and have it be a huge success, but I'm more worried that it won't be.*

- *I need this, but I don't want to pay too much for it.*

- *I don't want to get ripped off by someone who knows more about how this works than I do.*

The contrast is a stark one. While we go into a pitch with an opportunity mindset, the customer has a 'risk' mindset. Their thinking is problem-oriented and almost exclusively focused on what could go wrong.

Information is not the only currency

Back when sellers had a greater influence over what people bought, it was often because we controlled the information that was made available about our products and services.

This meant that anybody who wanted that information had to come to us, which gave us a lot of power.

But buyers, understandably, didn't like this so much. They thought it made us lazy and greedy.

So they invented procurement and professional buying, including the discipline of competitive tendering. Since the 1980s competitive tendering has been growing quickly. In the 2014-15 financial year, one of Australia's largest buyers – the Australian government – spent $59.447 billion on buying goods and services through its online competitive tendering system, Austender, and issued 69,236 supplier contracts.

At the same time, the internet – and social media in particular – changed the way buyers could access information. Now, it's very easy for buyers to find their own information, and to seek information from other buyers (or customers).

What does that mean for sellers and suppliers?

We've gone from a time where we had a lot of power, to one where we it doesn't feel like we have much power at all.

Throughout history, power has changed hands many times. Power is usually the province of those who control the resources – the things that we all need and want.

Back in ancient times, those who had the most power were those who controlled the food. In nomadic times, to be a hunter conferred great power and prestige. As we stopped moving around so much and started to settle into village life, farming became as important as hunting, and the feudal system was born. That's the reason why the great lords of Europe became so powerful; they controlled the land, which everyone else needed to produce food.

As sellers, when we held all the information, we had more power. Now we don't, and most of us don't know how to reassert our value. As a result, you may hear the following frustrations being voiced by people within your business:

- *Why don't customers understand how important this is?*

- *Why don't they 'get' us?*

- *Why do they insist on buying from that guy, who we know is not as good as us?*

- *Why do they insist on doing something that isn't going to get them the great result we know we could get?*

- *Why won't they listen?*

- *Don't they care?*

Actually, customers do care – but they don't care about us. Or our technical solution. Or our years of experience and impressive qualifications. At least, not specifically.

They care about one thing – themselves – and getting the results that *they* need to get. This isn't saying that buyers aren't nice people, or that they're not good to work with. It is just the pragmatic reality.

Money is not the only currency either

Buyers have always held the purse strings, but that doesn't give them ultimate power. Yes, they can choose, but not always from among alike things that will give the same result.

So, any time we have something unique and valuable that someone else needs and wants, we have power too.

For example, when restaurateur and celebrity chef Heston Blumenthal transplanted his celebrated Fat Duck restaurant to Melbourne during the shutdown and refurbishment of the original in Bray, England, the $525-a-head tickets were sold by ballot.

$525 is a lot of money and, given that there were 14,000 tickets on offer, you'd think that meeting this target would be kind of a stretch. But no.

Fat Duck Melbourne received 89,179 entries worldwide in the online ballot. Based on an average booking of three people per table, that equates to a staggering 267,537 people who couldn't wait to part with at least $525 a head – and with paired wines, nearer to $900 a head – to get a piece of the action.

At the time, the sought-after ballot was likened to the 'golden ticket' to Willy Wonka's chocolate factory, a fitting comparison for a man who is known for his fantastical food creations, including snail porridge, bacon & egg ice-cream, mock turtle soup and Meat Fruit. Dining at The Fat Duck is an experience you can't get anywhere else – and to a lot of Melbourne locals, the cost compared pretty favourably to the alternative – a trip to England.

Corporate and institutional buyers are also waking up to this idea that not all suppliers are created equal, and that they really need to do more if they want to get the best from us.

Category management – the process of standardising, rationalising and commoditising major spending categories – is now a mature discipline in procurement circles, and most buyers have gone through this process at least three times. This means that any big savings windfalls that may have been made from their supply chain have been long since gobbled up into past profit and loss statements.

Now, procurement leaders will need to shift their focus away from simply cost-cutting if they want to find new ways to create value from their supplier relationships.

As they turn their attention to other spending categories, such as services procured by internal clients within the business, procurement is experiencing some resistance and pushback. Unlike procurement, these internal clients don't have cost reduction as their primary aim – they want to buy insight, quality and outcomes.

In *The Procurement Value Proposition: The Rise of Supply Management*, Gerard Chick and Robert Handfield argue that much of the current approach to procurement tends to over-emphasise operational considerations, and underplay the commercial interests that exist in all business relationships.

As a result, they say, procurement people aren't thinking enough about the elements of value that are needed to sustain these relationships, and don't fully appreciate the complex, overarching tensions that exist between buyers and suppliers. This will come as no surprise to anyone who has ever lived the reality that these tensions inevitably create. Chick and Handfield go on to say:

> *Buyers often assume that they are in positions of dominance where they can simply instruct or command suppliers. However, the opposite is far more likely, and in the majority of buyer-supplier relationships the buyer would benefit from an enhanced understanding of the supplier's needs and wants.*
>
> *An understanding of the sources of supplier value could help buyers to manage a whole range of buyer-supplier interactions, and develop them to gain strategic competitive advantage.*

One answer, they suggest, is to develop 'solution-oriented bids', where the brief articulates the problem to be solved and requires suppliers to use their expertise to propose a solution. This sounds like an absolute no-brainer, but it isn't that simple, because the competitive tendering systems of today do exactly the opposite.

Notwithstanding this, the fact that experts on the supply side are now proposing this idea seems to recognise that its time has finally come. Buyers are starting to realise that when you tell an expert what to do, it is often at their own cost – the cost of the expertise the buyer could have benefited from if only they had asked for it.

As the buying process is disrupted, the way you sell will probably look very different. We are moving to a time when customers will actively seek your strategic contribution, and where everyone in your business needs to be involved in the work of customer value creation.

In the table below we can see how the evolution of the dance between buyers and sellers will affect the way we need to sell.

Fig. 1 The evolution of sales organisations

	THEN	NOW	NEXT
Environment	Competitive	Commoditised	Disrupted
Sales process	Sell on credentials	Sell on price and value-adds	Sell on strategic contribution
Sales problem	Convincing	Collaboration	Engagement
Supplier's key stakeholders	Technical/ professional/ operational	Sales & marketing	Whole of business
Outcome	Most experienced wins	Most cost-effective wins	Greatest value contribution wins

This change is coming, but to make it happen faster, we have work to do.

Firstly, we need to accept that not everything we would like to control is under our control. We can't control what competitors do or offer, and we can't control how customers choose to buy.

Secondly, we need to exert more control over the things that are within our control.

We can control what *we* do, how we think, what we offer, and how we show up to do it.

In the next chapter, we'll look at what it means to be in service of others, and how our intentions shape the results that we get.

CHAPTER 3

The power of service

TRAVEL IS WONDERFUL, BUT it can be chaos sometimes. We're out of our comfort zone and when something goes wrong, it can be hard to know what to do.

Recently, my family and I were on vacation in the USA and lucky to make it out of Charleston, South Carolina, where Hurricane Joaquin had caused widespread flooding. Nothing life-threatening, but potential chaos loomed for our travel plans, as the downtown area where we were staying had flooded.

It was a Saturday, and we needed to get to the car hire place by 12pm or we would be stuck for the next two days.

Uber had called it quits for the day, and one taxi stalled on its way to get to us. After a fraught couple of hours, we were lucky to be offered a ride by Steve, the front desk manager at the hotel who had just finished his shift. Steve dodged puddles and sped past roadblocks and emergency vehicles with their blue lights flashing, depositing us exhausted but thankful at the car hire place out of town.

While Steve was helping to unload our luggage, the rental manager was giving us a choice of two completely unfamiliar cars we could choose to take. In our frazzled state, we were ill equipped to make *any* kind of choice.

As our lizard brains tried to switch off 'fight or flight' mode to take in what he was saying, my partner asked the rental manager: "Which one would you choose?"

He didn't hesitate. "The Kia Soul" he said. "It's newer, higher and will give you more clearance if you hit any flooding on the way to Georgia."

Sold. Emboldened by his confidence, we made it out of South Carolina – and into Savannah, Georgia – successfully navigating several flooded roads.

That's the power of service.

When you're working with a customer, you have the opportunity to do far more than exchange time for money. You also have the chance to play a valuable role in their world.

In this chapter, we'll look at how customers, and our own attitudes towards them, can land us in unrewarding roles like servitude and subservience, and how rising above these roles is the first step towards our real goal – to be of service.

Servitude

Servitude is the state of being a slave, or completely beholden to the will of someone more powerful.

Other not-very-nice words that can be used to describe servitude are bondage, subjugation, domination and enslavement.

Spare a thought for the servants who worked in homes in Britain up to and including the Second World War. Life for them was pretty brutal, and not at all the way it has been portrayed in TV shows like *Upstairs Downstairs* and *Downton Abbey*.

In 1901, more than 1.5 million British people – one in four in the total population, and mostly women – were working as servants.

Servants tended to work seven days a week, often from as early as 5am until as late as 10pm, for very little money, all while doing demeaning things like clipping the master's toenails and ironing his shoelaces. To further help them to 'know their place', newly hired servants were often stripped of their real names and given generic names like Henry and Sarah. Employers rarely took pity on staff who were overworked, exhausted or ill – even if they were just children. And there wasn't much companionship either; most servants worked alone, as the only servant in the home of middle-class families.

You'd think we would be more enlightened in the 21st-century, especially in prosperous economies, and that servitude would be dead and buried.

But this is not the case.

Our buying system today is creating an underclass of servitude. Some businesses are being driven into the ground by unscrupulous buyers intent on wringing every last dollar out of them, and the people within those businesses live in fear of losing out, instead of in hope that their expertise and contribution can do some good in the world.

In this prosperous and enlightened day and age, that's just not acceptable.

If you are living in servitude – in any way, shape or form – we need to make that stop.

Subservience

Although slightly better than servitude, with all its connotations of fear, poverty and being trapped, subservience isn't a pleasant state to exist in either. Subservience erodes our professional pride and confidence, and left too long, can eventually turn into servitude.

Descended from the Latin, the term subservience originally just meant 'usefulness', and was associated with reasonably benign attributes like compliance and obedience.

But now, we have also come to associate subservience with less pleasant attributes, like submissiveness, inferiority and sycophancy (sucking up).

In a selling environment, subservience really means doing things that we don't want to do, or in a way we don't want to do them, and according to a set of rules and criteria that we didn't set and don't like very much.

For example, you might find yourself subservient in the way your performance is managed.

Who sets the Key Performance Indicators, or KPIs, in your contracts, you or the buyer?

Chances are it's the buyer, who has set out an entire service level agreement that they will require you to comply with. But you are the expert, and this work is something you do every day. You know, better than anybody, what constitutes an acceptable, good, or exceptional level of performance. It can be insulting not to be invited to participate in setting your own goals and targets – almost as if you're not trusted to work hard or do the right thing.

In the world of buying and selling, the procurement process is set up to make suppliers subservient. It's made clear that we are just an 'input'; one cog in a larger wheel, a means to an end, and that we are expendable and replaceable.

One example of this is where buyers come to us when they are already far along in their buying process. As a result, they will often ask us for something and we will immediately know it's not the right way to do it.

Unfortunately, by this point the buyer can seem pretty set in their approach, which makes it a bit tricky to explain this tactfully.

Maybe they've had an internal team working on it and this is their solution. Maybe they've sent us a Request for Tender demanding a compliant response.

"Oh well," we say pragmatically. "May as well give them what they want, or we risk not getting anything at all."

Subservience is the result of a power struggle, in which the 'master' exerts their power to get a result that favours them. It isn't always overt or obvious.

We see subservience at play in employer-employee relationships too. For example, the comedy *Horrible Bosses* plays on the rage that is created by long-term, long-suffering subservience in the workplace. It tells the story of Nick, Kurt and Dale, three ordinary guys who are subjected to ridiculous, over-the-top torture by the bosses they work for.

This includes being forced to drink whiskey at 8.15am, and losing a promotion because of it; being told to fire 'fat people'; and being barraged by a constant stream of sexual harassment. Too cash-strapped to quit, the three devise a hapless plan to murder each other's bosses, making each death look like an accident. This sounds awful, but it's a great movie if you haven't seen it.

The impression that subservience creates in a buyer-seller relationship is that what the seller does is not rocket science. Being on the receiving end of this kind of attitude can breed defeatism and anger among sellers, who just want to be trusted and valued for their expertise.

Service

Most of us probably don't give a lot of thought to what we really mean when we use the word 'service'. The word 'service' itself has become glib, overused and meaningless.

In business, the term 'service' has even become a category of complaint, rather than a category of endeavour.

That's a real *disservice*, if you'll pardon the pun, because service is the most noble of pursuits. To work in service of others is to build cities, make things happen and change lives.

Look into the term 'service' and you'll see a lot written about customer service. But this is really only the transactional element of a service offering – the tip of the iceberg. It's what goes on underneath that creates real value.

That's because service underpins every interaction we have with another human being, whether in a professional, friendship, family, or romantic context.

Being 'of service' is a deep-seated human drive that is related to our need to connect to other people.

This need to connect is as fundamental as our need for food and water.

In the book *Social*, social scientist Matthew Lieberman, says that we tend to assume that people's behaviour is narrowly self-interested, focused on getting more material benefits for themselves and avoiding physical threats and the exertion of effort. However, the research suggests otherwise – that in fact we are profoundly shaped by our social environment, and suffer greatly when our social bonds are threatened or severed.

So, the prospect you know you could really help never called you back. That initial meeting that went so well seems to have amounted to nothing. The 'urgent' proposal you put together over the weekend, instead of going to your son's basketball game, is languishing in an inbox somewhere. The tender submission you slaved over for a month didn't even get shortlisted.

When people reject our help, it doesn't just suck, it physically hurts.

Functional magnetic resonance imaging (fMRI) studies show that rejection piggybacks on physical pain pathways in the brain. In one study, participants who were given painkillers before being asked to recall a particularly upsetting rejection experience reported significantly less pain than those who took a sugar pill. Apparently, rejection sends us on a mission to destroy our self-esteem, lowers our IQ (at least temporarily), and does not respond to logic, even when we understand the reasons, which have nothing to do with us. Ouch.

Rejection creates social pain. And social pain is real pain. Because of the way social pain and pleasure are wired into our operating system, these are motivational ends in and of themselves.

Very few of us seek to connect with others just so we can extract money and other resources from them.

Instead, we want to be of service.

In business development commentary, you'll often see the word 'service' used interchangeably with other words, such as sales or influence. But they are not the same thing.

Service is a deep-seated need to be of use, to create, and to leave a legacy. Service is the 'pure' intention to create an outcome. Influence and sales are by-products and outcomes of the act of service.

When we act in service, we get to show up as the best and highest version of ourselves.

Service is the noble intention that breaks stalemates and gets buyers and suppliers working towards a greater, larger goal.

So, service is something to aspire to – not just something we do or deliver.

To serve or to deserve?

"We've worked hard. We really deserve to win this tender."

"Competitor A got the last job, and Competitor B got the one before that. It's our turn now."

"Our qualifications and experience speak for themselves."

"Our firm has a good reputation. Business should just come to us."

"We took a hit on that last project. Customer X really owes us one."

If you've heard these statements before – or maybe even said one or two yourself – you're in good company. We all feel these things from time to time.

There's no doubt that the grind of selling can get exasperating. This in turn can muddy our intention to serve, and also get in the way of learning when things don't go the way we hoped they would.

Also, our interpretation of what it means to 'deserve' has changed a lot over the years.

Originally, the word 'deserve' meant to serve zealously. Today, it usually means that we think we are entitled to something.

Thinking of 'deserving' by its original meaning, to serve zealously, is part of the mindset that helps us to making more successful connections and more sales.

Selling is really just 'helping'. That's why we call it service.

In the next section, Commoditisation, we'll look at the reasons why it can be so hard to be of service – and what we can do to overcome them.

PART 2

Commoditisation

Commoditisation has been the primary focus of corporate buying patterns for several decades, but this is changing. In this section, we'll examine the forces that still stand between us and the work we really want, and why it's essential to swim out of the "sea of same" to be valuable to customers.

CHAPTER 4

Swimming in the sea of same

WHEN COMPARING THE MARKETING and credentials material of organisations operating in some services industries, you could be forgiven for concluding that they were actually the same business, just trading under different names.

Consider the following (fictionalised) examples in the industries of engineering, human services, and IT services:

Engineering

We are an award-winning national engineering firm with a commitment to delivering high-quality projects. We maintain a unique employee culture that empowers our teams to deliver highly personalised, commercially viable and robust engineering solutions. With experts who sit on many of the industry's leading regulatory bodies, we are at the forefront of industry developments in engineering. We invest in the development of our staff, and our high-performance teams deliver exceptional client service that goes the extra mile for our customers.

Human services

We are a community organisation with a proud history of supporting marginalised and disadvantaged people, including children, young people, families, Indigenous Australians, people with disabilities, people from culturally diverse backgrounds, and older Australians. We deliver end-to-end services in urban, rural and remote communities that deliver on our vision of safe and strong families living in socially inclusive communities. We are working to create opportunities that break the cycle of poverty, improve people's quality of life, and give a voice to those who are most vulnerable.

IT services

We are an enterprise IT solutions business that works with our customers to create efficiencies across their people, processes and technologies. We believe in the power of information technology to drive business growth and innovation, and our team delivers unmatched depth and breadth of expertise with global reach. We will help you to leverage your existing IT investments by assessing your current systems for peak performance, delivering data hosting and business continuity solutions, and providing hardware maintenance.

Do any of these descriptions sound like your business? Do they look familiar in terms of the way you're accustomed to talking about yourself? And could they equally describe most of your competitors?

Industries develop a kind of 'common language' that helps professionals in the industry communicate with one another.

This is useful to a point, until it becomes a common marketing language as well.

The more that customers experience this common marketing language, the less differentiation they see – and the more likely they are to commoditise us.

It is understandable why this happens.

The more successful an enterprise becomes, the more others will want to emulate what it says and does.

This problem isn't exclusive to business; it's something that creative people across all industries experience.

Take Eminem, for example.

Eminem (Marshall Mathers) is one of the most successful hip-hop artists of all time, selling over 170 million albums since 1996. He grew up in a poor neighbourhood in Detroit with his Mum, and has exhibited a lifelong interest in storytelling. Before discovering hip-hop, he wanted to be a comic book artist.

One of Eminem's best-known songs, *Without Me*, was released as the lead single from his 2002 studio album – by which time he was already very successful. *Without Me* reached No. 2 on the U.S. music charts and No. 1 in many other countries worldwide. In it, Eminem talks about the many copycat artists that followed in the wake of his success:

> *Though I'm not the first king of controversy, I am the worst thing since Elvis Presley*
>
> *To do black music so selfishly, and use it to get myself wealthy*

Hey! There's a concept that works

20 million other white rappers emerge

But no matter how many other fish in the sea, it'd be so empty without me

And he's right. There really is only one Eminem that the world is going to remember. Vanilla Ice? I don't think so. At least, not for the right reasons.

If it feels like you're referencing a competitor in the way that you talk about yourself, customers will notice. Like the music-buying public, they see everything that is put out there for their consumption.

It is impossible to stand out and make an impact when you're swimming in the sea of same.

The paradox of procurement

There is no doubt about it; winning business can be hard.

It can take a long time to get an opportunity over the line. We can work very hard on something, and want it with every fibre of our being, and still find out at the end of the day that we are denied the prize.

It can seem so much easier – almost a relief – to have someone step in and take the responsibility of new business pursuits away from us, by telling us what they want to buy from us instead.

On the surface, that's what seemed to happen when buyers started to professionalise their buying practices, and the discipline of procurement began to emerge.

Some suppliers, much as they may argue to the contrary today, were kind of relieved when procurement came along.

Finally, here was a process we could follow. We would be told when opportunities were coming up. We could respond to those opportunities and win business that way.

Great, we thought. That relieves us of the responsibility of having to go out and get the business ourselves. We could lay off a few salespeople, sit in our offices and wait until opportunities came along.

But of course it wasn't long until we realised that this wasn't going to make things easier; in fact, it was going to make them a lot harder. We weren't the only ones being notified of these opportunities. So was everybody else in our industry.

Although few of us like it, the idea of competition has some merit. Genuine competition among a few, qualified equals can help us to sharpen our game and make our ideas better.

Compulsory competition, though – like what you'll find in the competitive tendering system – is different. Compulsory competition is designed to commoditise suppliers and to drive everything down to the lowest common denominator; its price.

This has three unintended effects on the buying system:

1. It has a demotivating effect on suppliers, who now see competitive tenders as an exercise in paperwork and not as an exciting opportunity to win new business. As a result, many organisations set up their business development

teams like a kind of 'bid sweatshop', putting junior people on the job and valuing quantity of submissions over quality.

2. It withers away a supplier's proactive business development effort, which relies on the creativity, energy and enthusiasm of the entire business – including people who are now doing something else with their time.

3. And finally, it stunts the work of value creation, which starts with suppliers but also benefits buyers, the community, and in some cases the world we all live in.

How are you cutting your cloth?

For a smart person who loves to help others through their expertise, the work of designing a program or a service delivery methodology is fun, and full of purpose.

When we have to decide how to cut our cloth to fit a customer's design, though, we are sacrificing our own inventiveness, originality and creativity – and with it the potential breakthroughs that would make a difference to us and to them.

Unfortunately, the decision-making network in our brain doesn't know how to prioritise important decisions over those that may be less important, or even meaningless.

In *The Organised Mind: Thinking Straight In the Age of Information Overload,* Daniel J. Levitin cites neuroscience research that asked participants to make a series of meaningless decisions – for example, whether to write with a ballpoint pen or a felt-tip pen. The more of these meaningless decisions they were asked to make in a day, the more they tended to show poor impulse control and lack of judgment. The need to face so many trivial decisions created neural fatigue, leaving no energy for making important decisions.

This is exactly what happens when we give over our lives to responding to briefings that have been created by someone else; for example, competitive tenders. Invariably, the requests they make will not fit the way we would choose to do things, meaning that our brains end up exhausted by the 'busywork' of making endless trade-offs and concessions to fit what we think that the buyer will want.

While we are focused on someone else's thing, we cannot focus on our own.

Attention is a limited-capacity resource, and our attentional systems have evolved to focus on only one thing at a time. In effect, by cutting off bits of ourselves to fit someone else's ideal, and exhausting our attention span in busywork, we are sacrificing our ability to think creatively.

In the competitive tendering system, nothing illustrates the futility of this pursuit more than sitting through a government tender briefing session.

Here's how it usually goes.

A government Department issues a Request for Tender, which comes with an information session. Sometimes, attendance at the information session is mandatory.

On the day, it's clear from the outset that the relationship between the buyer and the potential is not one of 'collaboration', nor is this a trusting environment in which real change and transformation is going to happen.

The buyer's team sits panel-style at the front of the room. They briefly tell you their name, and before you've even had a chance to scribble that down, they're off into their monotone delivery of a deck PowerPoint slides, which contain no information other than what is already available in the tender documents. No questions are taken until right at the end. Answers are often brief, or taken 'on notice'. Thanks to probity restrictions, there are no opportunities for a human conversation in case an aggrieved competitor might want to interpret that as favouritism.

As we suffer through this 'death by PowerPoint' and the bureaucrats hide behind their ancient laptops, many of us leave lamenting that we will never get those three hours back.

It is frustrating to sit through tender briefing sessions, and also kind of insulting. Supposedly, the purpose of these sessions is to help prospective bidders to get their heads around the tender document, and how they should respond. In reality, the tender request is often recited to us, leaving us with no additional information than we had when we read it through ourselves. Often the only real value of a tender briefing session is seeing who else is in the room and who you might be competing against (or, depending on your industry, could potentially collaborate with).

Over the years I've held dozens of sessions with a supplier's team to develop strategy for a tender response. I wish I had a dollar for every eye-roll, snort of derision, or howl of disappointment generated in these sessions, while the experts in the team are reading over what the buyer is asking us to do. I could have retired by now, and be sitting on the beach.

While experts rail against the buyer's proposed solution, often it's their definition of the *problem* that we really have an issue with. If only we'd been able to influence them earlier, we lament, we could have stopped them from wasting money; taking unnecessary risks; spending time they didn't need to spend; and generally making things hard for themselves.

Don't spend your life giving other people what you think they want. This is the equivalent of being trapped in the nightmare of the government tender session forever.

Unless we allow ourselves the time to build value for a customer, and for ourselves, it's probably not to happen. In the introduction to his book *In Praise of Idleness,* Bradley Trevor Grieve says:

> *Everything you admire, and everything anyone has ever created that inspires you is the result of their being able to step away from their pressing obligations and think really big – or really small, as the case may be.*

> *Consider the great and wondrous things already realised before you and I existed, and then imagine what might yet be accomplished if only we allow ourselves the mental space to conceive it.*

Unfortunately, there are reasons why we've ended up in the sea of same – and it isn't entirely our fault. In the following chapters, we'll look at the phenomenon of commoditisation, and other barriers to winning new business, and how we can break free of the constraints that limit our contribution and growth.

CHAPTER 5

The five forces driving commoditisation

AT THE MOMENT, WITHIN your business, there are probably three different kinds of work that you could be doing:

1. **Engaging work:** work you love, and want more of

2. **Routine work:** good, solid work that comes to you easily, pays the bills and keeps the lights on

3. **Marginal and painful work:** work that has become dull or uninteresting over time, is unprofitable, or difficult to deliver.

Fig. 2 What kind of work are you doing?

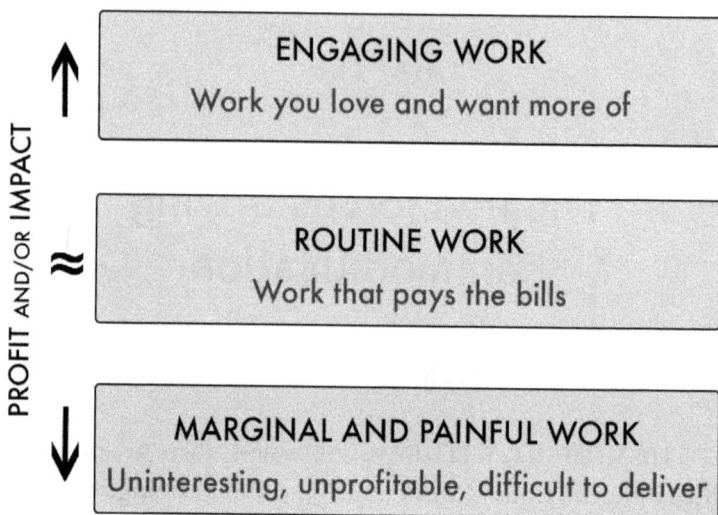

Unfortunately, many of us spend way too much time on the second two, and not nearly enough on the first.

That's because the way we run new business pursuits skews the result to deliver more of the work we *don't* want, without any of what we really do want.

Routine, marginal, and painful work is often the result of something we built and delivered a while ago, and that has now been commoditised to the point where buyers demand to get it cheaper and cheaper.

This leads to a problem experienced by most services businesses – shrinking margins. According to CSIMarket.com, the professional services industry is achieving net margins of only 11.24%, while construction services are at 7.31% and transport and logistics are at a meagre 4.55% – the result of commoditisation.

In financial markets, the term 'commodity' refers to primary agricultural products that can be bought and sold, such as wheat, coffee, cocoa and sugar, or raw materials derived from mining like gold, copper and oil.

Barring differences in quality, these products will all look – and perform – much the same.

When something has become commoditised, it means that buyers perceive an almost total lack of meaningful differentiation between the products or services in a particular category.

As a result, commoditised products are forced to operate on very low margins as they are sold on the basis of price, and not features, benefits or brand.

Ten years ago, Uday Karmarkar, writing in the Harvard Business Review, predicted the 'huge wave of change' bearing down on the services industry, one result of which has been commoditisation.

He identified Outsourcing/offshoring, Automation, Customer Self-service and Global Competition as the four forces driving this change.

To this, I will add one more – Isolationism – the growth of social, rather than in-person, interaction, and the way this makes our dealings with one another more impersonal and self-serving, and more likely to lead to commoditisation.

So here are the five forces driving commoditisation in services markets.

Force 1 – Outsourcing and offshoring

In order to cut headcount and overhead costs, many organisations have outsourced functions that they used to do in-house.

The main forms of outsourcing are information technology outsourcing; knowledge processing outsourcing (like research, analytics, litigation, and content development); and business process outsourcing (like payroll and call centre support).

Offshoring takes this to another level, by also moving the work to a country that offers a similar level of service but lower wages.

Despite the amount of discussion and fear generated by an increase in offshoring practices in Western markets like Australia, the OECD's research shows that jobs lost to offshoring account for only a small percentage of aggregate job losses (for example, less than 5% of total job losses in Europe) – far behind the job loss effect of bankruptcies, shut-downs and restructuring.

However, offshoring does have the effect of generating immediate and severe price competition, as wages in English-speaking countries that are the major beneficiaries of offshoring work – including the Philippines, Pakistan, and India – are significantly lower than wages in Australia.

On the plus side, there can be a timeliness benefit to organisations whose customers demand fast turnaround times. One of my clients, who works in the engineering field, has a drafting team offshore who can produce technical drawings at half the cost and also in half the time (from the customer's perspective, anyway) – because they work while we sleep.

Force 2 – Automation

Technology is having a major impact on services industries.

New developments in technology allow workers to be more mobile, and get more done in less time. Routine tasks like order taking and billing, that used to be performed by people, are now being performed by software instead.

Customers now expect that we are on top of the technology issue, and not just because they are enticed by what's new and shiny (although that's definitely part of it). Buyers see technology as a way to do things smarter, faster and better – and of course, much, much cheaper. Where technology improvements used to be a major plus in a new business pitch, increasingly they are just an expectation.

Force 3 – Customer Self-service

These days, we are living in a self-service world. And it seems most of us quite like it that way.

We would rather queue for an ATM instead of explaining ourselves to a waiting bank teller. There's a line for the self-service checkout at the supermarket, even while the aisle with the operator stands empty. We check ourselves in to a flight on our smartphones, weigh our own baggage at the airport and use a machine to print out bag tags. And companies are trying to come up with even more ways for us to 'help ourselves'.

Author Daniel J. Levitin points out that all this self-service actually means we are doing more work than ever before, as consumer organisations are offloading their work onto us.

Levitin refers to this as 'shadow work' – a kind of parallel economy in which a lot of the service we used to expect from companies has been transferred to us, as the customer. He also points out that this means each of us is now doing the work of others and not being paid for it, which is responsible for taking away a lot of the leisure time we thought we would have in the 21st century.

From a buyer point of view, as they face disruption and cost pressures in their own businesses, customer self-service shifts the costs onto the consumer instead of eroding their bottom line.

Force 4 – Global competition

While machines and workers in developing countries are increasingly capable of taking on routine service tasks, we are told that there is a pressing need to reinvent higher-order, sophisticated and brain-driven service provision in developed nations like Australia.

All well and good.

At the same time, we are facing aggressive competition from other developed nations, who are entering and disrupting our markets.

In 2013, French bus company Transdev won a $1.7 billion, 10-year contract to operate 30 per cent of Melbourne's bus network, edging out Victoria's largest local bus company Ventura. At the time of the win, Transdev promised to overhaul the bus routes it would operate, simplifying routes and increasing the hours of operation on weekdays and weekends. Cost savings were one reason behind the shift, with the new contract imposing penalties for late or cancelled services and tying bonuses and penalties to patronage growth.

Force 5 – Isolationism

Our one-on-one relationships are maintained differently now, and relationship building in business – and anywhere – is much harder than it used to be.

The rise of social media means that we are now very comfortable with online, rather than in-person, relationships. In business, personal relationships are now formed after we win the business, rather than before.

A study in the Scientific American found that empathy levels have declined steeply over the past 30 years, with a particularly sharp drop since 2000, along with a corresponding rise in narcissism. Probably not surprisingly, the turn of the century was around about the time when internet traffic and online relationship building really started to take off.

This doesn't bode well for the way we do business with buyers, who, like anyone else, are more likely to be impersonal and self-serving in their interactions with us when they don't know us very well.

And when they don't really understand what we do, either, they are more likely to perceive it as not very different to what someone else might do.

While the effect of commoditisation has left some businesses struggling to find new business opportunities, for others it's the complete opposite – at least on paper.

The lure of 'easy work' promised by advertised competitive bids and tenders keeps many people flat out just keeping up with the opportunities they feel they need to respond to.

This constant state of busy-ness leaves us struggling to find time to go after the work we really want, and frustrated that opportunities we know would be perfect for us, are passing us by.

Because we're responding to a buyer's briefing or agenda, we aren't doing our best work, nor are we capitalising on our strengths or vision.

And when we do win, we often end up with more routine, marginal and painful work as a result.

If, instead, you'd like to win engaging work that will sustain and energise you, it starts by thinking differently about how you pursue new business. But first, as you will see in the next chapter, there are a few other barriers we will also need to make our way past.

CHAPTER 6

Other barriers to getting new business

ASIDE FROM THE MORE global effects of commoditisation, there are forces closer to home standing between us and the work we really want.

These forces can be **internal** – things that come from inside ourselves – or **external**, such as the things that customers and competitors do and say.

For the sake of argument here, I will call these forces 'barriers'. There are three main kinds of internal barriers:

1. Practical,

2. Structural, and

3. Psychological.

And there are three main types of external barriers:

4. Access

5. Urgency, and

6. Competition

When your efforts to win new business are being frustrated by these barriers, they can seem larger and more substantial than they actually are.

These barriers are like poison – they slow us down and can even kill us if we let them. Luckily, there's an antidote for all of them. Let's take a look at the internal barriers first.

Internal barriers – Practical

Practical barriers may include lack of access to product information, marketing collateral, competitor research, or any one of a number of other things that we think we 'need' in order to get out there and talk to people about what we offer.

It can be hard to argue with practical barriers. After all, a thing either exists or it doesn't.

However, when our reluctance to 'do' business development is primarily about our lack of brochures, slide decks, white papers, and those sorts of things, what this really means is that we're not yet sold on what we are supposed to be selling.

The first sale is always to yourself. If you aren't sold, no one else will be.

In their book *Conviction,* Cook, Church and Henderson explain that it is more likely to be the person who is doing the selling that has objections – 'too pricey, don't need it, not now' – instead of the customer.

Instead of 'objections', they say, what customers actually have is:

- **Questions** – for example, "How will this work with our internal change program?"

- **Considerations** – for example, "What would happen if we swapped out this part with that part?"

- **Alternative options** – for example, "What if we did this ourselves?"

- **Time** – for example, "Is it urgent enough to do it this quarter, or should we wait until the new financial year?"

These questions, considerations, alternative options and time constraints are all things that we need to think about when building what we are selling, so we can be flexible and understanding when we get in front of a customer.

According to a study conducted by B2B research and advisory firm Sirius Decisions, up to 70% of content and collateral created marketing departments in business-to-business organisations sits unused anyway.

Practical barriers aren't really barriers – they are more like 'objections' we have to the idea of getting out there and talking to people about what we do.

The antidote to practical barriers is value: Worry less about how good your PowerPoint slides are, and think more about the value in what you're selling.

Internal barriers – Structural

Legendary management guru Peter Drucker said that the purpose of a business is to create a customer. But in practice, what many of us spend our time doing seems to run contrary to this purpose.

Structural barriers are things that we have created – usually for what seemed like a sensible reason at the time – that end up getting in the way of our business development success.

Here are a few examples:

- **Treating business development as a function, rather than a goal.** This is what happens when we employ a salesperson or business development person and expect them to carry everything, while the rest of the business sees their responsibilities as simply to 'deliver' on what they sell. This just doesn't work anymore. The work of business development is to create value that makes customers want to buy. Therefore, the most successful businesses are those where everybody in the business understands that they have a role to play. There's just no way that one person, or even a small group of people, can do everything that's necessary to create, present and deliver value for a customer.

- **Process for the sake of process.** Particularly in larger and older businesses, it's common to see processes that have been set up to suit the business, and not the customer. When someone says "this is the way we've always done things", it's a red flag that this is an area that has become internally focused and is probably detrimental to delivering value for an external customer. Processes should make things easier, but in fact often make them damned difficult.

You can probably recall a time when you were on the other side of the fence, as a consumer, negotiating with a business for something that took much longer and provoked more aggravation than it should have (making insurance claims immediately comes to mind).

- **The way we spend our time.** Most of us spend way too much time on things that actually aren't very important, and not enough time on things that are. How much of your day is spent answering email? In meetings? Completing reports? Resolving problems for other people? Now, how much of your time do you get to spend on actually building new things, and creating value for customers? When we spend all our time reacting to things, we're not creating anything new. And when we're not creating anything new, we are not building anything valuable for customers to buy.

The antidote to structural barriers is value. Take an honest look at your organisational chart and internal processes and ask whether your structure is inhibiting, instead of creating, value for customers.

Internal barriers – Psychological

Psychological barriers can come from a number of sources:

- A lack of confidence or self-worth, when we believe, deep down, that we're not really good enough;

- Comparisons to other people, including competitors; and

- The experience of loss and rejection, or a loss of Buoyancy, which can make it difficult to pick ourselves up and get out there again.

Confidence

In other people's eyes, confidence equates to competence. This, in turn, has a huge effect on our ability to turn opportunities into sales.

Let's say things are going well and you're winning everything that you pitch for. Chances are, confidence isn't really a problem right now. Winning gives us external validation that we are worth something, which leads to more and more confidence. Times are good.

Then all of a sudden, something changes. We lose one or two. Then the trickle of rejections turns into a flood. And all of a sudden we aren't so confident anymore.

There is a growing body of research showing that confidence is the *result* of competence; in other words, when we do well, we end up feeling good about ourselves. When we feel good about ourselves, we're prepared to push ourselves a little further, so we achieve more. And so the cycle goes.

On the flip side, if we don't do well, our confidence plummets. And when this happens in a profession where instant feedback, scrutiny and rejection are a regular part of the job, you've got a recipe for falling revenue and sales.

I once worked with a Sales Director who was on a mission to arrest his sales team's terrible losing streak, which had resulted in their confidence hitting rock bottom. What would fix it, he said, is if they could only experience what it felt like to win again.

To overcome a lack of confidence, we might try to 'fake it until we make it.' Although this is worth a try, unfortunately, it might not work too well.

According to Cameron Anderson, a psychologist at UCLA (Berkeley), extremely confident people genuinely believe that they are valuable, and it's this self-belief that is attractive to others. "Fake confidence just doesn't work in the same way," he says. No matter how much bravado we muster, Anderson explains, others will pick up on our shifting eyes, rising voice and other giveaways.

In 2009, Anderson undertook a study to find out why confidence leads to a perception of competence. He gave a group of 242 students a list of historical names and events – including some that sounded plausible, but were actually completely made up – and asked them to tick off the ones they knew. Some students ticked off the fakes as well as the real events, implying that they thought they knew more than they actually did. Afterwards, Anderson also asked the students to rate one another according to their social standing within the group. The students who had picked the most fakes also achieved the best ratings – in other words, those who had the strongest confidence in their abilities also had the highest social standing.

The antidote to lack of confidence is value. When you have done the work to establish the worth of what you're offering, it is much harder to shake your confidence.

Comparison

Comparing yourself to other people is doomed to make you feel bad. There's always going to be something – or someone – who seems to be doing better than you are.

Psychologists have coined the term 'social comparison theory' to explain how we determine our own social and personal worth by evaluating how we stack up against others. Apparently, we are constantly grading ourselves in terms of how we think other people are doing, often in negative ways. While these comparisons can be informative, they're almost always discouraging, because someone's always going to end up on the bottom.

However bad comparisons make us feel, we can't seem to stop doing it.

Psychologist Dr Deborah Carr studied the mental health of college-age students and found that many of their mental health problems could be attributed to the consequences of social comparison; the fact that they were comparing their own accomplishments, looks, athletic ability, academic results, or popularity to their classmates and feeling that they were coming up short. This is also referred to as the 'Facebook effect', an online environment where we are exposed to a constant parade of people who seem to be more popular and to be having more fun than we are.

In the study of college-age students, comparison was found to harm self-esteem and resulted in increased rates of depression, anxiety, and self-harm. It's not too much of a stretch to see that this would apply to the rest of us too, even though we may have clocked up a few more years on the planet.

If we knew the whole truth, Carr suggests, we might not feel so inadequate when comparing ourselves to other peoples' carefully crafted public images of 'perfection.'

"A friend may proudly announce the publication of their new novel, but conceal the 12 rejections their manuscript received before this," she says. "We may envy the smiling suntanned family we see on a tropical vacation, but we're not privy to the three hours of squabbling and sniping that came before that 30 seconds of smiling."

Unfortunately, constant comparison generates a kind of paralysis that is difficult to break free of.

It also turns out that comparison is a terrible way of judging something's actual worth.

Researcher and university professor Brene Brown, whose talks on vulnerability and shame are among the most popular on the TED platform, says that comparison is all about conformity and competition – which might seem mutually exclusive, but are not.

"When we compare, we want to see who or what is best out of a specific collection of 'alike things," Brown says. "The comparison mandate becomes this crushing paradox of 'fit in, but stand out!' It's not 'cultivate self-acceptance, belonging and authenticity'; it's 'be like everyone else, but better.'"

In business, when we evaluate ourselves mostly through comparisons to competitors who appear more experienced, more polished, or more productive, we omit something important – the customer's needs and experiences. In doing this, we are only seeing half the picture, because true value can only really be judged through the experience of the user.

Even more importantly, when we spend all our time looking at what competitors are doing and saying, we are wasting one of our most precious resources – time – that would be better spent creating something to benefit ourselves.

The antidote to lack of confidence is value, and value is unique to you. So it's important to run your own race. Switch off your social media, empty your brain of what others are doing, and build something you can be proud of.

Loss and rejection

Loss and rejection are part and parcel of the game in business development. But they certainly aren't pleasant, and our feelings about them aren't so easy to manage.

Rejection is common in new business pursuits. As we saw in Chapter 3, rejection doesn't just suck – it really hurts, because rejection piggybacks on physical pain pathways in the brain.

If you've ever lost something – or someone – who was important to you, then you've experienced the other half of this equation – **loss**.

Losses are emotional, not just physical. When we lose, we experience a complex range of emotions including sadness, sorrow, fatigue, depression, relief, shock, anger, guilt, and anxiety.

None of these emotions seem appropriate to express in a business setting, so we bottle them up. I call this 'unexploded grief', and I see it a lot in people who haven't really acknowledged their feelings about past business losses.

Pile loss on top of rejection, and you have a recipe for depression and anxiety, which can show up as 'call reluctance' and other forms of business development refusal and aversion.

Past business losses and rejections create scars. Without healing, these scars are obvious to those around us, and can be off-putting to the thing we really want – more connection, more customers and more sales.

I experienced the off-putting power of visible scars quite vividly last Halloween, when my partner and I went to a fundraising trivia night. Lacking the time to sort out costumes, we'd been to the two-dollar shop and bought a few packets of zombie temporary tattoos. These were pretty gory, including bullet holes, nails that were dripping with blood, and lots and lots of gashes and stitches.

We spent a fun hour or so applying them to our necks and faces, and then covering them up with grey and white makeup and some purple and green to make bruises.

The end effect was so scary that, when we stopped off at the supermarket to buy some snacks, I realised that I couldn't look anybody in the eye. Although it was Halloween, people looked absolutely horrified when they saw me.

Without realising it, many of walk around like this – with bullet holes, open wounds and scars – that are the result of past disappointments. We think that people can't see, and don't notice, but they do.

The antidote to rejection and loss is value. When we show up to help others, our focus needs to be on them – and not on proving something to ourselves. Rejection and loss are a lot

less likely when we've built value that proves our intention to be of service.

External barriers – Access

Now, this really is a tricky one – or so most of us think.

Everywhere, we see evidence that buyers don't want to talk to suppliers anymore.

A CEB study of more than 1,400 business-to-business (B2B) buyers revealed that 57% of a typical purchase decision is made before a customer even talks to a supplier.

Gartner Research predicts that by 2020, customers will manage 85 percent of their relationship with an enterprise without interacting with a human.

In this gloomy scenario, your emails will always go unanswered, the phone rarely rings and prospects never call you back.

But this isn't the full picture. People still buy things, and they still need information, but increasingly they want to consume it in the way they want, when they want, and without us needing to be involved.

This is the reason why content marketing has replaced the traditional face-to-face sales call in many B2B markets.

As well as the humble website, this means things like podcasts, whitepapers, case studies, apps, videos, online product demonstrations, LinkedIn groups, and regular publication of opinion and thought leadership.

The purpose of content marketing is to get enough of the right information in front of the right people so that when they're ready, you're the person they call.

The real barrier we have is not access to buyers – it's timing and language.

There are probably half a dozen people right now who have a problem that you can fix, sitting in meetings, on the phone or in their car right now thinking about it. But it's on their schedule, not yours. And they probably aren't thinking about it, or talking about it, in exactly the same way that you are.

The antidote to the access problem is value; understanding how buyers express the problems that you can solve, and when they are likely to be thinking about them.

External barriers – Urgency

If you have something that I need right now, I'll buy it. If not, you could be waiting a long time – probably forever.

If a buyer doesn't see what you're offering as a solution to a problem that is keeping them up at night right now, it will be very hard to sell to them.

With so many things on our to-do lists, it's no surprise that many of them get done only when they become pressing, or urgent.

In large businesses, most priorities are set well in advance. This means that the people we want to talk to have their world already set up the way they think they want it.

Also, like us, they are often beset by 'busyness', with their work (and life) one great rush from morning to night. This leaves prospects overstimulated and overtired. What we're offering is just one more thing that needs to fight for a place in their already-full schedule.

When something eventually does become urgent, it is often the result of market disruption.

Harvard Business Review defines 'disruption' as a process whereby a smaller company with fewer resources is able to successfully challenge established incumbent businesses.

As incumbents focus on improving their products and services for their most demanding (and usually most profitable) customers, they exceed the needs of some segments and ignore the needs of others. Entrants that prove disruptive begin by successfully targeting those overlooked segments, gaining a foothold by delivering more-suitable functionality—frequently at a lower price. Incumbents, chasing higher profitability in more-demanding segments, tend not to respond vigorously. Entrants then move upmarket, delivering the performance that incumbents' mainstream customers require, while preserving the advantages that drove their early success. When mainstream customers start adopting the entrants' offerings in volume, disruption has occurred.

Companies like Uber and Airbnb are good examples of businesses that started on a small scale, but grew exponentially by disrupting the prevailing business model in two established markets; transportation and accommodation.

Can you think of an example where disruption has happened to an organisation you had hoped to do business with? What was the effect on your relationship?

When markets are disrupted, we often feel the effects downstream in sales.

What seemed like a sure thing yesterday might evaporate today, as the customer restructures or battles an external threat to their own business.

The antidote to disruption is value. Customers will usually refer to an urgent problem as a 'priority'. By turning our attention to solving the actual urgent problem, rather than what we see as the problem, we are more likely to help the customer; address the priority; and land a sale.

External barriers — Competition

You probably don't really like the idea of competition and don't want to think of yourself as having 'competitors'. I've been in the business of competitive bids and pitches for a long time, and let me tell you – no one does.

When you're an expert, and specialised in what you do, it can be a shock to be in discussions with a buyer and suddenly find that you're in competition with other potential suppliers. This can be annoying, frustrating, and – whether you realise it or not – demotivating too.

Competition, whether we like it or not, is a fact of business life.

The discipline of procurement is set up to generate competition, and, where possible, force suppliers down to the lowest common denominator (price) through online auctions, quotes, and competitive tenders.

Procurement is the buyer's game, and many of us are forced to play it.

In the demotivating effect it has on us, external competition is a lot like the internal, psychological barrier of 'comparison'.

And as with everything we've spoken about here, the antidote to competition is value – when we can see the inevitability of competition as an opportunity to improve what we are doing.

And starting right now, we're going to do exactly that. Read on to learn how to change the game you are playing – and in turn, change your results.

PART 3

Value

Now, let's get to work. We'll discover the three drivers and six primary attributes that create commercial value for customers, and learn how you can talk about what you do so that customers want to buy it.

CHAPTER 7

Change the game, change the outcome

THE PRACTICE OF ALCHEMY is the medieval forerunner of chemistry. In medieval times, alchemists were occupied with the idea that it was possible to turn base metals into gold. This conjures up the image of a crazy wizard sitting in a cave toiling over steaming cauldrons of gloop.

But alchemy is also synonymous with the concept of creation and transformation.

Throughout history, alchemists have believed that when we change one thing, we can change our entire environment.

This sounds a bit like the plot of a sci-fi movie – the idea that changing one thing in the here and now could lead to a different future. Or, as Doc puts it in *Back to the Future*, "Marty! – Come back! Your actions could unravel the very fabric of the space-time continuum and destroy the entire universe!"

But in the real world, alchemy isn't the stuff of drama, explosions and apocalypse. None of us actually owns a DeLorean with a flux capacitor and the ability to go back in time, grab a copy of Grays Sports Almanac and get rich by betting on the winners in every game that has ever been played.

The basic rule of alchemy says that between you and anything you might want to influence, there's a relationship. When either party in a relationship changes, the relationship itself is also changed. That change in the relationship affects both parties.

So if we want to change something – like our win rates, sales results, the type of work we're winning, or its quality – the first thing we need to do is to discover the true nature of our relationship to it. Then we will be able to see how to change it by changing ourselves.

This section of the book is based on this principle; that by changing ourselves, we can change the nature of our relationship with buyers in a way that benefits us both.

The exchange of commercial value in business should be exactly that – an exchange. It shouldn't be a win/lose proposition, with the buyer winning and the supplier taking a beating.

It's not about who controls the agenda any more.

It's about what the agenda *is* – both sides have lost sight of this, and we need to bring things back on track.

Rediscovering why

When we're in the services business, we spend most of our time talking about 'how'; our methodologies, our service delivery models, our implementation and risk management plans, and our quality assurance processes.

What we don't talk about enough – or even think about enough – is *why*.

In his classic leadership book *Start with Why*, Simon Sinek says people don't buy what we do; they buy why we do it, and that what we do simply proves what we believe.

Your 'why' is your purpose; the reason you do what you do. Most likely, you discovered this a long time ago – during your training, study or early career – and it's as natural to you now as breathing.

But it's not natural for your customers, who have a completely different 'why' and who won't understand yours, unless you can explain it to them.

Sinek explains that there are really only two ways to influence human behaviour: you can manipulate it or you can inspire it.

Manipulation really doesn't work that well, especially now, when it's easier than ever to find out whether something (or someone) is above board through checking social media.

We have always trusted the recommendation of our families and friends over anything that a company might want to sell to us, and now it seems we are willing to extend this trust to total strangers too.

A study by Socialnomics showed that 90% of people using social media trust peer recommendations, but only 14% trust advertisements. Another study, by Social Media Week, showed that we trust the recommendations of website reviews (54%) almost as much as the opinion of professionals (58%) – both of whom are likely to be total strangers.

We are far less likely to trust the opinions of people when we know they are being paid for them, though. The Social Media Week study showed that bloggers who were paid to post a review are trusted by only 45% of buyers, but trust leaps to 76% when they aren't paid – even though we know that they did receive a free product.

It seems we're always on the lookout for credible sources of opinion about products and services – whether they are good or bad. Recent research shows that 58% of customers are more likely to tell others about their customer service experiences than they were five years ago, and a Harvard Business Review study showed that while only a quarter of customers are likely to say something positive about their experience, almost two-thirds are likely to speak negatively.

This is a difficult environment for sellers to manipulate.

The best chance we have of influencing others in this environment is not manipulation – it's inspiration. But inspiring others is almost impossible unless we are inspired ourselves.

The source of this inspiration is our purpose.

Let's go on a mission to excavate your purpose – your 'why' – which through years of doing what you do has probably been buried under layers of methodology and practice.

Why do I do what I do?

That's a good question, and one that I get asked quite frequently.

For most of the past 20 years, I've worked with organisations on high-stakes bids and tenders. This means deals involving huge expectations, tight deadlines, big dollars and many stakeholders, and often with many livelihoods at stake.

This creates a lot of pressure, is stressful and scary, and it's fair to say that being immersed in this environment is not most people's idea of a rocking good time.

So why do I do it then?

Here is a little interview I did with myself, to explain why I do what I do. I hope that this will help you to think about why you do what you do, and to answer these questions yourself.

Why did I choose this field? What difference did I hope to make? In the beginning, it was just about winning one deal at a time. But then it became about something bigger than that; helping people who do great work to do more of it, and to make the difference that our world needs them to make.

What gets me up and out there in the morning? I love seeing the lights go on when these smart people – who often don't think they can sell, and don't see it as their job to sell – realise what an enormous impact they can make by sharing their insights more generously with the customers who really need them.

What keeps me going when things get difficult? When you look at it mechanically, the work involved in a large, multifaceted bid can be difficult and demanding. But come to think of it, so is most worthwhile work, when you break it down to its mechanical parts. What keeps me going is the knowledge that that there are people relying on me to get them through this, and that I can help by breaking things down as clearly as possible.

What do you absolutely love about what you do? In the work I do, I get to be a kind of 'professional appreciator' of the amazing things that smart, creative, driven people can achieve. And for those who need a bit of help, it's a privilege to help them discover the possibility of what they could achieve if only they looked at their business, and their market, and their customers a little bit differently.

Why do *you* do what you do?

Now it's your turn to have a go at this exercise. You can write your answers, type them, or record yourself talking about them. I find this last option the most helpful, because it's more spontaneous and natural, and doesn't take a lot of time to do.

- Why did you choose the field you're working in?

- What difference did you hope to make?

- What gets you up and out there in the morning (apart from the need to show up and collect a pay cheque)?

- What keeps you going when things get difficult?

- What do you absolutely love about what you do?

When you're finished, review your answers. Does this sound like the real you? Are you inspired by it? Do you think others will be too?

Rediscovering your 'why'– and then putting it in terms that customers can understand, and taking them on a journey to appreciate it too – is essential to framing the commercial value in what you do, and getting others to invest in you.

The problem is the solution

Yes, buyer-supplier relationships have changed.

We can see this as a problem, or see it as an opportunity – knowing that when we change ourselves, we can change the outcome.

Productivity writer Paul Sloane says that if we are given unlimited resources to solve a problem then we can always come up with something – and often it is expensive and over-engineered. On the other hand, when we have to use the limited set of resources contained in the problem and its immediate environment, we are forced to be more creative – and very often the result is a solution that is elegant, inexpensive and effective.

Sloane cites the example of two prisoners who dug an 80-foot tunnel from their cell to escape from prison. In such an elaborate escape plan, the big problem was where to hide the enormous amount of dirt that was generated by all the digging.

So where did they eventually decide to hide the dirt? Back in the tunnel of course. Here's how they did it.

The prisoners stole nylon sacks from the prison bakery, and after digging the tunnel, put the dirt in the sacks. At cell inspection times they pushed all the dirt bags back into the tunnel and tidied the cell. After their escape, the guards found a cell full of bags of dirt and an empty tunnel.

This plan is brilliant, because it's so simple. The problem was the solution. The dirt had come out of the tunnel; so the solution was to put it back there. In solving this problem, the prisoners had very few resources – but one of them was the tunnel itself.

We have resources too.

Selling is a two-sided activity. It can often seem like it's one-sided, but it isn't. It's not just up to suppliers to produce and create, while buyers consume and critique.

Belonging and contribution are deeply felt human needs. We all want to be part of something and to make a difference. The work we do is one way of achieving that.

Although this book is about business development, it's not specifically about 'sales'. It's about engagement and connection.

The role of business development is simply to build value that customers want to buy.

There is an opportunity right now for smart service providers to stop struggling to walk the path we think customers want us to walk, and start creating our own destiny.

There is thought and work involved – certainly more than sitting and waiting for a tender to cross your desk – but it's the most worthwhile work you will ever do.

CHAPTER 8

The work of business development

THIS BOOK IS ABOUT business development, and business development is not 'sales' – or even marketing.

Somewhere along the line, though, the terms have become interchangeable.

- The purpose of business development is to build value that customers can buy.

- The purpose of sales (and marketing) is to go out and sell value, once it has been created.

When we are wondering why a sales or marketing effort hasn't been successful, it is often because we aren't investing in business development – we aren't making a concerted effort to build commercial value that customers can buy.

Our sales and marketing teams are often forced to trade on credentials and experience – things that our business has already built or done – which will deliver diminishing returns over time.

Credentials or obituary?

Reading the credentials of some businesses is like reading an obituary for a person who has already died.

Take a look at yours and see if you can spot what I mean. Are you talking a lot about the great things you did a long time ago? Does it sound like you work in a vibrant, growing business? Or one that's in a holding pattern or slow decline?

Customers are buying who you could be tomorrow and, and if it's going to be a long relationship, in three or five years' time. They are interested in what's coming next – what you're working on, investigating, tinkering with, and investing in.

Credentials are the price of entry to a conversation with a customer, but they're not the conversation itself.

A customer might agree to see you because they're interested in what you've done in the past, but it doesn't mean you're a slam-dunk to do the same thing for them.

Also, having a conversation about your credentials is a little weird. It's uncomfortable; it can make you feel like you've suddenly arrived at a cattle call audition for a Broadway show wearing a big fat number on your back.

For me, being asked to list my credentials at the start of a meeting with a potential customer is my least favourite way to start a conversation.

It feels like a job interview, and for a job I haven't even decided that I want just yet.

Now let's think about a situation that you may have experienced from another perspective – the 'buyer's' side.

If you've ever had the need to fill a job vacancy in your organisation or in your team, you've probably had to interview many people for the role.

Think back to that time for a minute. You're interviewing someone you will be working with every day. This person could mean the difference between getting results (or not) and making your life easier (or not). You're asking them questions, they're answering, and you are forming an impression about them.

At the end of the interview, who do you want to hire – the person who talks only about the work they have already done, or the person who has a vision for the work they want to do next – and how that will help you?

When we're hiring in expertise, we want to hire someone who sees their best years as still being ahead of them. That way, we get the full benefit of their potential.

Customers are conditioned to ask suppliers about their credentials, which is why we think that *they* think our credentials are important. It's the equivalent of polite party conversation: "So what do you do?"

We also have a tendency to believe that our good work in the past lends us some kind of magical halo that will float us away to success.

But others don't really know our history, they don't care and they pay far less attention to this than we think they do. As Matt

Church from Thought Leaders Global says, often, "You don't matter, they don't care and they're not listening".

Ever since I was a little girl, I've sung in musical productions and in choirs. I was lucky enough to play the lead in a number of school and community shows until my mid-twenties, and even to sing the American National Anthem at our high school's homecoming basketball game while I was an exchange student in Kentucky, USA. At the moment, I'm singing in a women's pop choir.

A couple of years ago, my choir was preparing for a new show and there were some opportunities to audition for small group and solo parts. I was secretly excited about the opportunity to try out for these, but I put off thinking about it and as a result I didn't really prepare anything to audition with.

On the day of the auditions, our choir director called people up in small groups to sing for the parts. My own audition was with a group of four others, and was over in less than a minute. Afterwards, our director thanked everyone and told us that all who auditioned would get the opportunity to sing something. Although I knew I had been a bit underprepared, I was relieved about this and felt pretty happy that I had stood up and had a go.

Two weeks later I was on the Gold Coast delivering a presentation at a conference. On the way back to the airport in the taxi, I pulled out my phone and saw a message from our choir director, with the list of all the people who had won parts.

Eagerly, I scanned the list to see which part I was going to be singing, but my name wasn't on there. I looked again.

I hadn't misheard her, surely? She did say that everybody who auditioned was going to get a part? Yes, she had mentioned this again at the start of her email. But no matter how many times I read that list, my name still wasn't on it. It was like I hadn't even been there. Ouch!

Right now, my history and experience as a singer didn't matter one little bit. What did matter was that I didn't really show up that day and show what I could do. I went in lazy and unprepared, and might as well have been invisible.

Every day, we have this choice in our professional lives. We can rest on our laurels and hope that somehow, someone cares or remembers, or we can make the best damn show that we possibly can today.

The problem with unique selling propositions

For a long time, the world of marketing was very taken with the idea of unique selling propositions. The idea was to find the thing that's unique about you, compared to other people in your market, and position yourself on that.

This sounds like a reasonable idea, but I reckon it's wrong on four levels:

1. **It encourages us to look externally for validation,** by comparing ourselves with competitors. As we have seen, this is often a fruitless exercise with negative psychological effects.

2. **It's very superficial.** A unique selling proposition is often something that just skims the surface of what you do; it's an attention-grabber, rather than a deal maker.

3. **It uses the word 'selling'.** Business development is about creating value, and selling is just the transactional bit that follows on from that. Selling isn't a function in itself, especially now, when it's all about supporting customers to buy.

4. **Finally, just because it's unique, doesn't make it valuable.** The world is full of unique things that no one bought, including Jell-O for salads, toaster bacon, and blue French fries. (All real products that tanked horribly. Kind of a shame about the toaster bacon though).

What we need to find is your unique *value* proposition, not your unique *selling* proposition.

Transcending competition

"That's all very well," I hear you say, "But we do have competitors. We want to be better than them. We *want* to be unique."

The aim for any business is to be so great at what we do that, essentially, we have no competitors. Customers are drawn to work with us; they love what we do; they stay with us for the long term.

In delivering services, it can be quite challenging to arrive at this position, not least because it's usually the customer who is dictating the terms of our contracts and our service-level agreements.

When you break them down to their constituent parts, most supplier/customer relationships are quite transactional.

We do things; they buy things. We build things; they receive things. The objectives are operational and functional.

The goal of a new business pursuit is to find the transcendent point; to identify a big, gnarly problem we can solve, or a goal that we can achieve, and to pursue this in partnership with the customer.

This means that instead of being locked in a struggle to the eventual death of the relationship – comparing our list of things we can do, with the list of things that they want, with the inevitable mismatched result – we are taking flight on a journey that transcends the mundane and transactional and achieves something of real value for both of us.

Sound like a big ask? It isn't really.

When buyers and sellers don't connect it is usually because we have two different people with two different agendas, essentially having two different conversations.

To get past this stalemate, we need to be able to very quickly move to a place where we are addressing the bigger, more important questions for both of us:

What's the bigger agenda here?
What is really at stake?
What is the higher purpose that we are trying to serve?
What's the most important thing that, together, we could achieve?
What should we really be talking about?

These questions always result in better conversations than those that are just about, "Here's the need that I have, and here's the credentials you might have to fill it."

What do customers really want?

This is a tantalising question.

But like the Holy Grail, the answer to this question can be frustratingly elusive. There are many reasons why this is the case. Here are just a few of them:

- **Personal differences.** Like you and I, customers are complex beings. They don't all want the same thing. It doesn't matter if they have the same problems, are in the same industry, or work for the same company.

- **Changing priorities.** Even the exact same buyer may want one thing one day, but something else the next.

- **Invisible forces.** We can never possibly hope to know everything there is to know about another human being. We can't see everything that's going on inside their world or their head.

People have tried many things to overcome these problems; asking customers what they want, forensically examining a customer's mission and vision statements for clues, and telling them what other customers have done in similar situations. Some of this can be useful, to a point. But these approaches are not without their problems.

For example, have you ever bought a present for a loved one who admired something in a shop window, only to find that when you give it to them, six months later, they have no recollection of it and it's pretty clear that they don't really want it? This happens to my partner all the time – with me – and apparently it is very frustrating!

Market research can be a bit like this.

It turns out that market research (asking customers what they want) is a poor predictor of what they will actually buy. According to AcuPoll, as many as 95% of new products introduced each year fail. Time Magazine lists the top 3 product failures of all time as the Ford Edsell (1957), which cost $2.9 billion in today's terms; the Hewlett Touch Pad (2011), which was discontinued almost immediately at a cost of $885m in assets and $755m in wind-down costs; and Crystal Pepsi (1992). All were backed by expensive market research and extensive marketing campaigns.

We need to figure out what customers really value, not just what they say they want.

And now, we're going to do just that. In the next chapter, we'll unpack the three primary drivers of customer value, and discover how you can leverage them.

CHAPTER 9

Value drivers

WHEN CUSTOMERS THINK ABOUT buying from you, they are sizing you up with these questions:

Are you the real deal?

Will you give me what I want; help me figure out what I need; and take me to a place that's better than where I am now?

Buyers don't really commoditise suppliers. We do that to ourselves, by not giving them the criteria, options and information to make a better choice.

What is value?

Price is easy to understand, which is probably why we default to it so often.

'Value' is much harder. Value is both a subjective and objective concept. It exists in tangible and intangible form.

Warren Buffet once said, "Price is what you pay, value is what you get". While it's a simple idea on the surface, there's a lot to this concept of value.

Traditionally, businesses look to their purchasing or procurement departments as a way to increase their profits, usually by cutting costs. As a result, suppliers are constantly under pressure to reduce prices, often to achieve arbitrary procurement targets such as 'a 12% cost reduction across the board in the current financial year'.

It's frustrating that customers expect prices to only ever go down, when we know that the opposite is true. In Australia, the Consumer Price Index (CPI) measures changes in the price level of a basket of consumer goods and services commonly purchased by households. In recent memory, I've never heard of this going down – it goes up every year (although it may fall during a severe recession).

As suppliers, if we want to get our customers to think about value, we need to educate them away from the blunt instrument of comparing solely on the cost of acquisition – the price they pay when they initially buy from us. To get them to have this conversation with us, we need to have an accurate understanding of what our customers value right now, and might value in the future.

Unfortunately, the way we run new business pursuits makes it hard to have this conversation. When we wait until customers tell us what they want, and then, like everyone else, try to give it to them for the lowest price, we are robbing ourselves – and them – of a more valuable conversation.

There are a lot of different words we can use instead of the word 'value':

- Advantage

- Benefit

- Efficacy

- Gain

- Merit

- Worth

- Usefulness

- Utility

When we turn these over in our minds, we can see that one thing they all have in common is that they are highly subjective, personal and individual.

Value exists in the mind of the recipient; the person who benefits. Therefore, no two people will see or define value in exactly the same way.

What creates value for me probably won't represent value for you. That's because we have different hopes, dreams, goals and problems to solve.

Value is like a snowflake.

You've probably heard it said that no two snowflakes are exactly alike. However, whilst snowflakes can form into a huge variety of intricate shapes, every snowflake has six sides. This 'radial symmetry' occurs due to the crystalline structure inherent in the formation of the snowflake.

As a result, although snowflakes are all different, they aren't a great, amorphous, unrecognisable mess either.

Snowflakes have a six-sided structure.

Value has structure too – and like a snowflake, it has six sides, and is quite beautiful when you can see it up close.

Because value exists in the mind of the recipient – the customer – the attributes or categories we assign to value need to sound like things they would actually say.

Unfortunately, this often isn't what happens.

Looking for a definition of value in business, I found this one in the Harvard Business Review:

> *Value in business markets is the worth in monetary terms of the technical, economic, service, and social benefits a customer receives in exchange for the price it pays for a market offering.*

That's all very well, and it sounds reasonable.

But would a customer define value this way? Would they actually say any of these things if you asked them what attributes they value?

Probably not.

Creating value is, by definition, a creative process, and these aren't very creative words.

They sound like the culmination of something, rather than the beginning. And it is devilishly difficult to work backwards from an endpoint to get a result.

So, like Julie Andrews in the Sound of Music, let's start at the very beginning – a very good place to start – by thinking about the things a customer might say if we asked them to make a list of the things that they value.

We'll ask them to do this by completing the sentence, "I want it to be..."

So, their answers will go something like this:

1. ...*safer.*

2. ...*cheaper.*

3. ...*simpler.*

4. ...*faster.*

5. ...*smarter.*

6. ...*better.*

These are the six main value attributes we will be exploring in the rest of this book.

Think of each of them as 'buckets' or categories that can contain an infinite variety of elements, which will vary a lot depending on the customer, your business and your industry.

You will be filling and emptying these buckets regularly, based on what you already have available to sell, and what you will be creating or building.

In the way that these attributes are expressed – 'safer, cheaper, simpler' and so on – each one also implies a relationship to something else, or a comparison with another alternative.

This is exactly what buyers are doing when they are comparing what you offer with their other options – doing nothing, staying with their current supplier, or going with you.

We can never forget that customers have a choice. So whenever we are thinking about what we offer that might fit any of these attributes, we need to think about the alternatives as well:

- Safer than....

- Cheaper than...

- Simpler than...

- Faster than...

- Smarter than...

- Better than....

Value and 'values'

Our values are the things we hold dear to us; the things we believe are non-negotiable, maybe even sacred.

Your values will underpin every decision you make and every aspect of how you live your life.

Whether you're aware of if or not, you will have your own set of values, and your organisation probably has a set too. Hopefully these are similar to your own (or at least not too far apart).

Most organisations work with a set of about five core values, which are simple and easy to remember. Some examples of core organisational values might include:

- Collaboration

- Customer focus

- Ethics

- Hard work

- Honesty

- Innovation

- Integrity

- Ownership

- Personal development

- Professionalism

- Recognition

- Respect

- Risk-taking

- Safety

- Teamwork

- Trust

- Work-life balance

When people go into a pitch or competitive tender, and they don't have a previous relationship with the buyer, something they will almost always do is to search out the buyer's list of published values and try to figure out how their product or service embodies these.

While that's not a bad idea as a starting point, there are two problems with this approach.

- Many corporate value statements espouse what organisational development consultant Patrick Lencioni calls 'permission-to-play' values, which simply reflect the minimum behavioral and social standards required of any employee in any kind of organisation, and don't distinguish them from others operating in their industry. Customer focus, teamwork and honesty might be examples of permission-to-play, or generic, values. These are not particularly helpful in disginguishing your service offering from a competitor's.

- On the other hand, some corporate value statements are actually a series of aspirations, rather than descriptions of actual behavior that you can observe within the organisation. In some organisations, for example, values like collaboration, innovation, and work-life balance might represent what they would like to be – rather than what they are today. Pointing out where people are failing to live up to their stated values is a pretty slippery slope for an outsider. Get it wrong, and you'll be out on your ear – no matter how good your offer is.

As a result, corporate values statements can be a bit of a minefield for a supplier who doesn't yet understand the organisation very well.

Watching what people do, rather than what they say, is a far better approach because it gives us clues about what they are really valuing right now – as opposed to what they say they value.

After looking at the customer's published values statement, find some recent news about them, check out their place of work, and ask around your network. Do they say they value innovation, but are downsizing their R&D department? Do they say they value work-life balance, but in practice people are routinely in the office until after 9pm? Do they say they value safety, but have outdated vehicles and safety gear?

This will give you a better idea of what they really do value, as opposed to what they say they value.

Value judgments

A value judgment is a subjective assessment of the rightness, wrongness or usefulness of a thing or a person, based on some sort of comparison. In other words, a value judgment is a statement of what we believe.

For example, I believe that books are more important than sports.

Clearly, this is a value judgment that says more about my values than about the facts. There's no real way of comparing books and sports, other than as alternatives to how you might choose to spend your time.

I might choose to substantiate this value judgment by saying that kids who love reading have good imaginations, that they are good spellers, and that they find it easier to amuse themselves than kids who need a posse of people to be entertained and distracted.

But why malign sports in order to pump up the pursuit of reading?

The fact that I was hopeless at sports, and spent my Saturdays as a child on the side of a cricket field reading a book while my brother tore up and down making runs might have something (OK, a lot) to do with this particular value judgment.

But now you know this about me, you'll have far more success in selling me a membership of a book club than a season pass to Saturday-night football games.

Creating commercial value

Understanding what customers truly value is the only way to sell anything, to combat price pressure, and to avoid becoming a commodity.

There are three main drivers of commercial value that support the six attributes we identified earlier.

These drivers are **visceral, logical and aspirational.**

Each one exists on a different plane; is experienced in different places in the body; has a primary internal and external context that drives it; and plays a different role in the buying process.

Fig 3: The three drivers of commercial customer value

	Visceral	**Logical**	**Aspirational**
Level	Primary	Secondary	Tertiary
Body relationship	Gut	Head	Heart
Feeling	Fear	Need	Want
Buying attributes	Safer and Cheaper	Simpler and Faster	Smarter and Better
Environmental driver	Disruption	Information overload	Impact and Legacy
Buying role	Overcome resistance to change	Anchor practicalities	Think bigger and broader

The Visceral driver

When we have a 'gut feeling', we are experiencing a very strong internal reaction to something that's going on in our external world.

The gut has its own nervous system – the enteric nervous system. There is a primal connection between our brain and our gut, which are joined by an extensive network of neurons and a highway of chemicals and hormones that constantly provide feedback about things like how hungry we are, whether or not we're experiencing stress, or if we've ingested a disease-causing microbe.

Dr Deepak Chopra, a famous self-help author who also happens to be a neuroendocrinologist, has said that gut feelings are "every cell in our body making a decision".

Gut feelings can be physically felt, but not always logically explained.

For example, I'm convinced that Diet Coke saved my life.

Many years ago, my partner and I were about to head off on a road trip for a beach holiday with some friends. It was a beautiful day, and we had a lot to look forward to at the other end of the long trip, but for some reason I had a strong sense of danger and was very nervous about getting in the car.

We made it a fairly long way before we need to stop for lunch in a small town just outside a set of mountain ranges. So far, so good.

Due to my (at the time) pathological need for Diet Coke, and the inability of some of the town's few shops and cafes to provide it, we were delayed by a few minutes whilst we hunted it down.

When we finally did get back on the road, the traffic about 5km out of town was at a complete standstill.

Eventually, we learned that there had been a head on collision not very far ahead of us. It turns out that in the traffic coming from the opposite direction, there was a driver who was towing a boat. This being only the start of the Christmas holidays, they had forgotten that they had the boat on board when they made the decision to overtake a slow-moving vehicle on a narrow stretch of road. Unable to pull back in time, the boat had collided head on with a family travelling in the opposite direction. Everyone in that oncoming car – which was in our lane of traffic, only a few minutes ahead of us – had been killed.

The primary feeling related to the visceral plane is fear.

Here, I was reacting to a set of circumstances that existed in my environment, but that didn't necessarily impact me directly. The feeling of fear came from my gut, and was persistent and hard to shake – until we were on the other side of that accident.

In a buying setting, the visceral attributes that the buyer will identify – Safer and Cheaper – stem from their fear of loss.

At our core, we are all animals, albeit fairly sophisticated ones. What's visceral is instinctive. In business, not enough of us are 'tuned in' enough to this powerful source of buyer value.

- **Don't go without a visceral element** – Pitches that lack a visceral element can fail because there's 'no pain'. At least in the initial decision, most buyers are powerfully motivated to move away from pain (more than towards pleasure).

- **Don't go visceral in isolation** – Without logic and aspiration to balance them, the visceral aspects of value can seem intrusive, presumptive, aggressive or mercenary. But when combined with the other two levels, they help to overcome a powerful source of objection to change.

The Logical driver

Logic is the primary language of business and commerce.

Logical value drivers provide an anchor to the world of common sense. When we look at the world logically, we're said to have our feet on the ground, not our head in the clouds.

You'd expect that when we have a logical case for why something needs to be done, it would get done – straight away.

Unfortunately, this isn't always the case.

Logic is driven by the head, and most of us have way too much going on in there to be logical about all of it. This phenomenon is known as 'cognitive load'.

A heavy cognitive load has been found to result in something called Fundamental Attribution Error, which is essentially our propensity to blame others and their personality when things go wrong rather than seeing a broader range of factors that might have caused the problem.

For example, imagine you've arrived at the hospital to visit a friend only to find that the last two parking slots have been hogged by a single car that has parked right across them. You're late, stressed and there is no parking available in the surrounding streets.

You'd probably be pretty annoyed by this, and the Fundamental Attribution Error might lead you to think that the driver of the other car is selfish, inconsiderate or 'on drugs'. What if, instead, you knew that the driver was a man whose wife was giving birth in the front seat? You would probably then realise that he had a pretty good reason to park hastily, even though it doesn't make up for the fact that there's still no space for you to fit your car in.

Buyers fall victim to Fundamental Attribution Error and the pitfalls of a heavy cognitive load in the same way we all do.

In a buying setting, the logical attributes that the buyer will be thinking about – Simpler and Faster – come from the context of need.

Prioritising all the things buyers 'need' to do takes work and effort. That's why there is value in someone else (you) helping them to make that decision.

- Don't go without a logical element- Pitches that lack a logical element can fail because there's 'no rationale', or no business case. This makes it harder to justify the change, despite the fear of loss (the visceral element) and the allure of something 'sexy' (the aspirational element).

- Don't go logical in isolation – Without aspiration and visceral drivers to balance them, the logical aspects of value can seem sterile, over-intellectualised, expedient or glib. Done in combination with the visceral and aspirational aspects, however, they help to anchor the practical aspects of a deal and put the wheels in motion.

The Aspirational driver

By definition, something that is aspirational is something that we decide that we want.

Consumers are motivated by three higher needs: affiliation, aspiration, and identity. Business customers are consumers, and they want these things too.

Wants are different to needs. They are things we'd like to have, as opposed to things we 'have to have'.

In theory, wants are easier to forego than needs. But not really.

We don't expend a lot of our energy thinking about how to meet our needs, which are mundane and often repetitive. But we do give a lot of energy to the things we really want.

How else to explain the value of luxury brands like Louis Vuitton and Prada? $2 billion spent each year on lottery tickets? $525 per person limited-time-only meals by Heston Blumenthal?

Wants are powerful, because when we can create a want, we have the ability to set someone on a different path to the path they might choose on their own.

You might have heard the expression "the heart wants what the heart wants". This appears to be an adaptation of an earlier saying from the writer Emily Dickinson, who actually said "The Heart wants what it wants – or else it does not care".

In a buying setting, the aspirational attributes that the buyer will take to heart – Smarter and Better – come from the context of want.

Smarter and Better are different in important ways. Better requires a baseline – a means of comparison to something that already exists. Smarter implies a whole new category of value that the buyer may not have thought of yet, but could be guided to – by you.

Aspirational value drivers are like a travel brochure for a luxury river cruise – they sell the beauty of the journey, as well as the destination.

- Don't go without an aspirational element – pitches that lack an aspirational element can fail because there's 'no gain' that buyers are excited enough to push for.

- Don't go aspirational in isolation – Without logical and visceral drivers to balance them, aspirational aspects of value can seem over-blown, puffed up, flowery, or fanciful.

Presented in combination with the visceral and logical aspects, though, they help to elevate the more mundane aspects of a deal and get everyone thinking bigger about what can be accomplished.

Let's now look in detail at the six attributes that sit behind these drivers, and how you can leverage them to build an offer that is so commercially valuable your prospective customers would be crazy not to buy it.

CHAPTER 10

Visceral value drivers: Safer and Cheaper

VISCERAL VALUE DRIVERS ARE the most fundamental, basic value drivers.

As we saw earlier, what's visceral is instinctive. Many suppliers tend to underestimate the importance of visceral value drivers as part of a buying decision.

Because we live in a culture where information is freely available, we're often tempted to try to do things ourselves, and often underestimate how difficult it will be.

A friend of mine, let's call him Scott to protect his dignity, once bought a fancy trampoline for his kids for Christmas. This brand of trampoline is known for its special jump space design that doesn't have exposed springs for kids to get themselves tangled in.

Thinking to save the $100 installation fee, Scott decided he'd put it up himself. Two days before Christmas, he unpacked all the bits and pieces and got stuck into it. After struggling for six hours, Scott was forced to call it quits, but not before making a midnight call to his dad to come over and help him the next day.

Early the next morning, Scott and his dad tried again. Even with the two of them pulling as hard as they could, they just couldn't get the springs to fit. After a few more hours of struggle, Scott pulled a muscle in his back and was now in serious pain. Plus, it was now Christmas Eve. In desperation, he called about a dozen trampoline installers he found online. Due to the time of year, all were booked and unable to help.

Eventually, after putting out a final desperate call to his network of friends, Scott found an installer who could fit him in. Finally, the trampoline was up, and just in time for Christmas.

Everyone was happy, except for Scott. His DIY attempt eventually cost him almost $1,000 in installation fees and physiotherapy bills – ten times what it would have cost if he'd gone for the professional installation service the manufacturer offered when he bought it. And that doesn't even take into account the pain and suffering.

Value attribute – CHEAPER

Category: Cost

Fundamental buyer question: How does this help me make the most of my money?

Fortunately for us, there aren't too many people who wake up in the morning and think "Gee, I wonder who I can rip off/cheat/ swindle today?"

Unfortunately, this truth doesn't get a lot of airtime in the dance between buyers and sellers, where cost is usually one of the most fraught and challenging issues we will encounter in making a deal.

Buyers seem to always want things cheaper. They're suspicious that we might be ripping them off. They're back and forth with their requests for a 'best and final offer'.

We're slighted and offended by the implication that we're only out for ourselves, and exhausted by the game-playing. This goes round and round in circles and gets us nowhere.

In a new business pursuit, "How much does it cost?" is almost always one of the first questions you'll be asked, often before you have enough information to formulate an answer. Although this can be confronting at first, there are three main reasons for this.

1. **We carry the same colour money in our wallets.** Of all the things that go into making up an offer or a deal, cost is the one that is the most universal and easiest to understand (at least in theory). As consumers, we all understand the value of money and are able to make instant trade-offs in our head – "Wow! That's 50 pairs of shoes", or "Geez! That's as much as a Maserati/Jeep/Lexus" (insert your favourite car brand here).

2. **Costs are easy to compare – at least in theory.** Once a buyer has seen a number, they're mentally totting up the value in their heads, comparing it with the value on the page and deciding whether the investment is worth it. Unfortunately, buyers often get this calculation wrong – simply because they're not making an informed comparison. This is one

reason why I always suggest you put your pricing at the back of a written proposal – not at the beginning.

3. **Costs have either been budgeted for – or not.** Understandably, buyers can be nervous about investing too much time and energy in something that might be outside their ability to pay, whether that's just at the moment – or at all.

As a commercial value category, however, 'cheaper' is a gold mine.

Everything has a cost.

There are things the customer is doing or not doing now that are creating costs, and that you can eliminate for them.

There's the cost of going with what you are offering (the investment or the fee), and then there's the cost of not going with it.

So cost is about a lot more than just the purchase price. In helping a buyer to understand exactly what it costs them to do – and not to do – what you're proposing, you are actually helping them to do business better.

Your role in discovering the value of 'cheaper' is to articulate the value in how what you're proposing will reduce or eliminate costs – many of which the customer may be completely unaware of.

There are two basic types of cost in business. First, there are fixed costs, which every business incurs whether we do something or not. Fixed costs are what help us keep the lights on and the doors open.

Then there are variable costs, which go up or down depending on the activity of the business. Variable costs make people nervous, because of their potential to get out of hand very quickly.

What someone is buying from you could represent either a fixed or a variable cost, depending on what it is and how they are paying for it.

There are also a few other ways to think about cost in the context of buying what you're selling:

- **Acquisition cost.** This isn't just a fancy way of saying 'price'. In management accounting, the Total Cost of Acquisition means all the costs associated with buying goods, services, or assets, including the net price (what you charge) plus anything else that's needed to get the item to the point of use, such as legal fees, implementation costs, or transportation.

- **Opportunity cost.** Opportunity cost represents the value of choice; what the customer could have done instead of what is actually being done.

- **Administration cost,** or how much it costs to manage something on an ongoing basis. Administration costs can be significant, and are often under-represented and not well understood within a business.

As a society, we value people who are 'good with money'. The investor Warren Buffet, at time of writing, was estimated to have a net worth of $60 billion, with Forbes ranking him the 13th most powerful person in the world. Yet Buffet is famous for being frugal. He still lives in the house he bought in 1958 for $31,500 in Omaha, Nebraska. He doesn't own a yacht or any of the other trappings of wealth, and when he married for the second time (after being widowed) chose to hold the wedding at his daughter's home instead of a fancy wedding venue.

Buffet is often quoted as saying: "The first rule of investing is don't lose money; the second rule is don't forget Rule No. 1."

Your job is to help the customer feel like they're Warren Buffet – a savvy investor with an eye for a bargain.

Here are some questions to ask yourself that identify how what you do helps the customer to do things 'cheaper':

- What's the customer doing or not doing right now that is creating extra cost, including costs they may not be aware of?

- How will the customer's costs directly benefit from what you are proposing? Will they see a direct cost reduction (price reduction or headcount reduction)?

- Is there any indirect cost benefit, i.e. a knock-on effect to other initiatives or other parts of the business? How, and what is that worth to them?

- Will their staff productivity increase? What's the value of that?

- Will they get better asset utilisation? What's the value of that?

- Will they see less wastage? What's the value of that?

- Will this help them to create revenue or make more money? How, and how much?

- How is this better than the next best alternative – the opportunity cost?

- What is the cost of not acting or changing?

- What is the cost of changing over to you? How could you minimise those costs?

- Is there any ongoing cost, or will you be removing ongoing costs? How?

Value attribute: SAFER

Category: Risk

Fundamental buyer question: How does this help me to minimise the risk that something will go wrong?

Risk is a very real consideration for buyers, and you will probably find that risk is at the heart of many of the objections customers have to buying from you.

Unless there's some kind of pressing need or emergency, making a move requires courage. It can feel safer to do nothing.

A recent study on sales execution trends by Qvidian found that only 63% of salespeople actually make their targets, with pursuits ending in 'no decision' the major reason for the shortfall. While four in 10 salespeople thought that an "inability to effectively communicate value" might be behind their lack of success, only half of them also chose this as a skill they needed to work on.

In their book *Insight Selling*, Mike Schultz and John E. Doerr present buyer research that shows that buyers tend to perceive risk in four categories:

- Seller – getting the buyer to believe, and believe in, the salesperson (and their team)

- Offering (product or service) – getting the buyer to believe the offering will perform as described

- Company – getting the buyer to believe the seller's company is the right choice, and

- Outcome – getting the buyer to believe he or she will achieve the promised results in an acceptable timeframe.

Here, though, we're looking at risk in the context of how it relates to creating *value* (not objections) for customers.

There is value to be found in identifying, communicating, managing and eliminating the risks that the customer faces.

This can include financial risk, operational risk, strategic risk (uncertainties and untapped opportunities embedded in the customer's strategic intent), governance/compliance risk, or risks to reputation.

Another way to think of the work you're doing is as a kind of 'insurance policy' that protects the client against things that could go wrong. Insurance isn't the sexiest topic, but it is a huge industry – in Australia, it is worth $58b a year and employs more than 22,300 people.

Insurance is something people understand, and although they may not like it, they are prepared to pay for it.

Here are some questions to ask yourself that identify how what you do helps the customer to do things 'safer':

- What's the risk of doing this?

- What's the risk of not doing this?

- What risks does our product/service help the buyer overcome?

- What is the cost or implication of these risks?

- Are these risks mission-critical for the buyer? In what way?

- How would the buyer rank the importance of these risks?

- Is the buyer unaware of, or underestimating, any of these risks?

- How does what we offer help the buyer to remove or overcome a risk?

- What is the value in doing that?

- In what ways can we limit the buyer's risk in doing business with us? Can we offer cost ceilings, guarantees, or accreditations?

By now, you'll be starting to get a picture of how your offer helps customers to do things Cheaper and Safer.

In the next chapter, we'll explore the logical value attributes – Faster and Simpler.

CHAPTER 11

Logical value drivers: Simpler and Faster

Logical value drivers come from the context of need and are ruled by the head.

Helping buyers to prioritise all the things they need to do, and to do them more quickly, has value because it relieves them of work and effort and helps them to be more productive.

Value attribute – SIMPLER

Category: Complexity

Fundamental buyer question: How does this help me make sense of the world?

Leonardo da Vinci once said, "Simplicity is the ultimate sophistication".

As an expert, one of your superpowers is pattern recognition and simplification. All the things you already know will help you to see things that other people can't.

This superpower helps your customers make sense of the world, cuts through their information overload issues, and offers them a different perspective than they might be able to come to on their own.

Watch a spider spinning a web and you'll see simplicity in action.

Spider webs are simple, beautiful structures, and they're a wonder of natural engineering. Spider webs are also enormously strong, though not, as commonly thought, as strong as steel. A spider web's unique strength is due to its combination of strength and stretchiness. The basic material of a spider web, spider silk has a characteristic way of first softening and then stiffening when pulled that enables it to resist localised damage.

An expert's brain – your brain – is a bit like this too.

Our current era in civilization, the period from the 1970s to today, has become known as the 'Information Age'. For this, we can thank mathematician Claude Elwood Shannon, whose pioneering work at Bell Labs between 1941 and 1972 laid the groundwork for the introduction of the computers that have changed our world.

Or we might decide not to thank him. For all the advantages that computers have given us, there are disadvantages – and the biggest one is information overload.

Gartner research recently estimated the total number of computers sold worldwide to be 4,187,000,000, of which 74% are sold for business. In 2015, tablet computers outsold desktop and laptop computers for the first time – 320 million to 316 million. And of course, if you're into squinting, you can check things out on your mobile phone any time you want. 1.95

billion mobile phones were sold in 2015, of which 70% were smartphones.

Within these little devices exists the potential for a never-ending stream of information coming at us 24 hours a day, 7 days a week.

So the age of information has quickly become the age of information overload.

In 1970, Alvin Toffler coined the term 'information overload' when he predicted that the rapidly increasing amount of information being produced would eventually cause problems. Information overload is an increasing problem in modern workplaces, where the issues this has generated include:

- **Volume.** The need to wade through enormous amounts of data to find what we need.

- **Veracity.** The difficulty in discerning the true, useful or insightful information among the sheer mountain of stuff we face every day.

- **Distraction.** The reward centres in our brains are fired by dopamine and thrive on novelty and new information (also known as 'shiny object syndrome'). This means it's practically impossible to focus on statistics about computer sales when there's a pop-up add promising pictures of "25 Photo Bombers Who Absolutely Nailed It" bobbing up and down in your attention zone. (That's not just me, right?!)

- **Exhaustion.** There's just no way of getting on top of all this data. In a five-year projection of how we use mobile devices, Cisco discovered that in 2014, the world sent 30 exabytes of data across the internet, or 30 billion gigabytes. By 2019, thanks to smartphones, tablets, wearables, video, and the Internet of Things, we'll send nearly 300 exabytes over the internet – an tenfold increase in only five years.

Feeling overloaded yet? I know I am.

Another emerging term to describe information overload is 'infobesity'.

The contrast in these terms is really interesting. 'Overload' is something that just happens to us on response to an external force we can't control. Unfortunately, the term 'obesity' has more judgmental connotations – that somehow we are responsible for this excess of information.

We are beginning to understand that being weighed down by excess information isn't healthy or desirable. When we know that this is happening, most of us are desperate to get rid of it.

When I ask my clients to put themselves in their customer's shoes, and to estimate how much of that customer's mental energy is expended on thinking about what they do for them, their answers are pretty confronting.

The response is usually somewhere between 1% and 20%. The truth is probably a lot less than whatever number they come up with.

Our 'thing' – whatever it is that we do – occupies a huge amount of our own headspace.

Our world is 100% fascinating to us. We think about what we do all the time. We live, breathe, and sleep it. We write speeches, books and papers about it.

Because of this, it's easy to overestimate our own importance, and forget about all the other things that are going on for a customer outside of what's in our own heads.

In behavioural science, confirmation bias is the tendency to look for, favour and recall information in a way that confirms our existing beliefs, while giving a lot less attention to alternative possibilities.

Confirmation bias contributes to overconfidence. In my experience, this is probably one of the main reasons why incumbent suppliers fail to retain business that they have assumed is theirs for life. It's easy to look for reasons that confirm the absolute invincibility of what we are doing already, rather than go searching for holes, gaps and opportunities.

When you are pursuing new business, though, confirmation bias is a major advantage.

These holes, gaps and opportunities may be small and hard to see, especially for someone who isn't an expert. The incumbent, whether that's a competitor or the customer themselves, is programmed to think that what they're doing is already good enough.

As an expert, your ability to see the big picture, to flex and stretch, and to cut through the mental clutter is valuable. The work you have already done to synthesise and make sense of a huge amount of information, and to find the holes, gaps and opportunities, is work that your customers don't have to do themselves.

Here are some questions to ask yourself that identify how what you do helps the customer to do things 'simpler':

- How does this simplify a complex issue for the client, in a way that makes sense without losing meaning?

- What are the essential things they need to know and do? What can they ignore or defer?

- How is the process simpler than what they're doing now?

- How is it easier? Are there fewer steps involved, fewer decisions, fewer people?

- How is this simpler for the customer to manage? Will it take up less of their headspace, and fewer hours in their day?

- Does this work within the customer's existing policies/ procedures/constraints without the need to make changes?

- Does this resolve some other internal problem that is creating 'noise' or aggravation for them?

- What opportunities are created when we simplify things for the client? What will they be able to stop doing? What will they be able to do instead, that is of higher value to them?

Value attribute – FASTER

Category: Productivity

Fundamental buyer question: How does this help me get through my enormous list of big, important goals?

Productivity isn't a new idea, with its roots in the Industrial Age and the need to measure and improve the output of people sweating away on a production line.

Labour productivity is also a measure of economic activity, and often cited as a reason why people should be paid more (or less).

In the Information Age, productivity is still important, because we are all struggling to achieve more with less – less time, fewer people, and very little leeway to make mistakes.

Corporate restructuring, which started as a knee-jerk reaction to bad economic times in the 1980s and 1990s, has become a mainstay of contemporary business practice, and 'downsizing' or 'right-sizing' of the workforce is a central component of this.

Many corporates, governments and large businesses restructure their workforces regularly – once a year is not uncommon.

In change management terms, those who are affected by downsizing are divided into three categories– executioners, victims and survivors. From our perspective, we are most interested in the latter category, the survivors, as they are the ones who are likely to be buying from and working with us.

Research into the impact of downsizing has found that those who retain their jobs in a restructuring are often asked to do jobs they are untrained or ill qualified to do, and that the threat of further downsizing can lead the most able employees to seek employment elsewhere. You've probably also noticed that people go on 'mental strike' as soon as a new restructure is announced – jockeying for position, worrying about their jobs, or lobbying for a redundancy.

'Survivors' of a restructure are more likely to have lower morale and increased stress levels, be less productive, less loyal, and display a higher propensity to quit. What this means in practice is that survivors are left trying to stretch themselves across multiple roles. This includes survivors in management and leadership roles, who are often left in a position where they need to juggle multiple people reporting to them across multiple line responsibilities.

Downsizing also leads to the need for outsourcing, when specialist roles no longer exist within an organisation. You probably know someone with particular skills who has been retrenched or made redundant, only to be 'hired back' in a consulting capacity when the employer quickly figures out that they can't function properly without them.

Another unwanted – and often unanticipated – effect of downsizing is the effect on innovation.

Innovation is essential to build a business and to create customer value, and it is much more likely to be achieved by a diverse workforce than by one that has been stripped to the bone.

Researchers collated a dozen or more studies on the effect of downsizing on innovation and found empirical evidence suggesting that the innovative capability of an organisation is likely to be harmed by downsizing, which:

- Conflicts with the goals of innovation

- Reduces available skills

- Breaks entrepreneurial networks

- Stifles risk-taking and flexibility

- Breeds a culture of fear, and

- Damages creativity and learning capacity

The survivors who remain in an organisation recognise this, and are increasingly looking to outside experts – that's you – for ways to plug their productivity and innovation gap.

As well as the increasing need to do more with less, and to innovate while we're at it, another reason why 'faster is better' is that we are all trying to accomplish way too much.

When you ask someone how they are these days, the most common response you'll get is, "busy".

One of my clients, the Chief Operating Officer of a large human services organisation, gets 400 emails a day. This is not all that uncommon, when the average office worker receives 121 emails a day, expected to rise to 140 a day by 2018.

In the book *I Know How She Does It,* Laura Vanderkam analysed 1,000 days worth of hour-by-hour time logs kept by working mothers earning at least US$100,000 a year, with an interest in finding out how these 'successful' women are spending their time.

What she found was surprising. Like all of us, the women in Vanderkam's study had 168 hours each week to work with. On average, they worked 44 hours per week – much less than they estimated. They slept 54 hours a week – much more than they estimated, at almost eight hours a day. This left 70 hours for other things, including having a life as well as an important job role. All the evidence seemed to contradict the 'endless juggling' and 'little or no leisure time' that many or them were complaining about.

Vanderkam is sympathetic to the reasons for this.

"I think that saying 'I'm busy' is a socially acceptable way to say 'I am important,'" she has said. Whether at work or at home, being busy shows that we are in demand. As Vanderkam points out, saying you get enough sleep is admitting that the world goes on without you – and where's the social reward in that?

Under pressure to get results daily, monthly and quarterly, the pace of life for your customers is probably relentless – or at least they'll want you to think it is.

Because of this, one of the objections you'll probably get to whatever you are offering is that prospects are too busy to consider it.

However, time is money. What you are able to do might actually be the key to helping customers to do things faster; to get on with other things on their to-do list; or to reclaim some of their personal time and balance.

Here are some questions to ask yourself that identify how what you do helps the customer to do things 'faster':

- How do we get things done faster than competitors?

- How is it faster than the client could get it done themselves?

- What are the tools and techniques that we use to streamline things?

- Are we able to deliver ahead of schedule?

- By doing this, will the customer be able to see quicker results or response times?

- Is there an accelerated or faster payback period?

- How does this enable the client to be nimbler, more flexible or responsive to change?

- How will it free up time in their schedule? How much? What is the value of this?

- In what other ways does our approach value the customer's time?

By now, you should be getting a good a picture of how your offer helps customers to do things Simpler and Faster.

In the next chapter, we'll explore the final set of value attributes – the aspirational attributes of Better and Smarter.

CHAPTER 12

Aspirational value drivers: Better and Smarter

ASPIRATIONAL VALUE DRIVERS ARE 'tertiary' value drivers, because they sit above – and come after – we have thought about the other two.

Aspirations are ruled by our hearts, and once we've decided that we want something, we give a lot of energy to pursuing it.

For suppliers, this means that when we can create a 'want', we can also set our customers on a different – smarter and better – path than they might be able to choose on their own.

Value attribute – BETTER

Category: Quality

Fundamental buyer question: Why is this an improvement on what is happening now?

Originating in manufacturing, the term 'quality' technically means to be free of defects, deficiency of variations. This requires adherence to certain standards that deliver repeatability, consistency and uniformity.

When we talk about quality, though, what we usually also mean is that our offering has some element of excellence, or superiority over alternatives.

Quality management is a well-established business discipline, with suppliers paying hundreds of thousands of dollars each year to be accredited to quality standards like ISO 9001. Often people moan about the cost of doing this, because it has become a basic expectation – the price of entry to winning large customers – but doesn't really add any value to a sales conversation.

Also, real quality can be difficult to pin down, particularly in the delivery of services.

When you look at a typical 'quality' process for the delivery of a service, what you'll often find is an emphasis on repeatability, consistency and predictability, rather than excellence or superiority.

For example, when I review an organisation's quality process for the delivery of bids and tenders, what I usually find is that the process has been modelled on the current practice in use within the business, rather than what might be considered a 'best' practice. In other words, it's based on what is usually done to get a proposal out the door – get this approval, run this checklist – rather than on the replicating the steps taken to achieve a successful result (bids that result in wins).

This mismatch between intent and delivery offers many opportunities for experts, like you, to quickly recognize and represent what can be done 'better'.

Better is a state that we all aspire to.

In *Drive – The Surprising Truth About What Motivates Us,* Dan Pink suggests that the true drivers of motivation are autonomy (the need to be in control); mastery (the need to stretch ourselves in pursuit of something we value); and purpose (feeling essential or part of something).

Asylum seekers and refugees, when asked to talk about the reason why they have fled their country, often talk about what they are moving 'towards'; a desire to create a better life for themselves and their families – rather than the more obvious things that they are clearly moving away from, such as war, persecution, natural disaster, food shortages, and other hardships.

As consumers, when we trade up to a new car, phone or sound system, it's usually because we think we are getting something 'better'. Whether it really is better or not can only be confirmed through experience, but to make the move, we are often convinced based on a list of attributes that seem to stack up much more favourably against what we have now.

Consumer goods companies understand this well, and will often sell their wares with a checklist showing the attributes of competing alternatives (short, bland) against the attributes of their own products (long, impressive).

Whether these lists work or not depend on whether the items they are comparing are items we value.

Health insurance extras are a good example of this.

For years, health insurance extras were sold on a list/comparison basis, until the range of optional extras became so large that the comparison became largely meaningless.

With the overall cost of health insurance going up, the cost of extras was also increasing.

For most healthy people who take out health insurance, and who aren't in hospital regularly, the extras are actually the point; they represent the main benefit we get back from our contributions each year. But health insurance extras policies return notoriously little for each visit, and also have low ceiling limits, say $200 for each category item. A couple of visits to the massage therapist and you've blown your rebate for the year.

Mentioning this to my massage therapist, a while ago, he let me know that a number of his clients had moved to a different insurer, who had combined the extras limits so that their customers could spend it on whatever they liked. At time of writing, and depending on the package, this insurer offers customers between $550-1100 a year to spend on whatever extras they liked without the interference of the insurer.

This is a great idea, and it's a good example of a supplier understanding how their customers would like to see things made 'better' – in this case, by removing the artificial rules, and therefore increasing the flexibility and value of health insurance extras.

In a business-to-business context, we can also see examples where 'better' has driven a buying decision.

Recently, one of the large facility management companies in Australia lost its 31-year contract at a major sporting stadium to a much smaller competitor, who employed only 6,000 staff nationally compared to its 30,000.

In making the announcement, the customer mentioned how they had valued the winner's investment of time and thinking about how to revamp their 70 bars, restaurants, hospitality suites and overall customer experience – in other words, how they could do things better.

What you're selling is a journey, as much as it is a destination. The journey starts when you can engage buyers and help them to visualise a different and better way of doing things.

Here are some questions to ask yourself that identify how what you do helps the customer to do things 'better':

- How is this better than what the current supplier is doing now?

- How is it better than what the customer is doing now (if there isn't a current supplier)?

- How is it better than doing nothing?

- How is it better than waiting? Is there a chance that some kind of change could actually render the problem even more urgent than it is now? What and how?

- How is it better than what the customer's market competitors are doing?

- How is it better for the customer than what the guy down the hall is doing (nothing like a little inter-departmental competition)?

- Why will this make a difference to the customer? In what way is it causing a frustration now?

Value attribute – SMARTER

Category: Connectivity

Fundamental buyer question: How will this make me look like a hero?

Smarter implies a whole new category of value that the buyer may not have thought of yet. This is exciting, and creates a wonderful opportunity for you, as their supplier, to influence them and to provide real and meaningful improvements in their world.

You and your team will often be pitching to people who have a much lower level of specific expertise in your service offering than you do.

This creates an opportunity to educate and inform – things that experts love to do.

We are no longer pushing products to customers, but inviting them to participate in the creation of products that they want to see – a process known as 'co-creation'.

In business, co-creation leverages the combined brainpower of you and the customer to come up with smart ideas that work specifically for them.

This is the essence of service, and the pinnacle of creating value for a customer.

Connectivity is a force that is re-shaping the way we buy and sell, with instant and far-reaching effects. In this context, connectivity means connecting ideas – 'connecting the dots' – and seeing possibilities that no one person could create alone.

For example, in consumer markets, companies like M&Ms, Nutella and Coke are inviting customers to define their brands through the creation or selection of personalised or self-named products.

This has a brand-building effect in a market where there are many copy-cat products.

- Personalised M&Ms cost US$29.99 a pound, making them four to five times the price of regular M&Ms. This doesn't stop people lining up around the block to buy them, and when in New York recently, we saw dozens of people clutching personalised bags while browsing through the giant M&Ms World concept store.

- The *Share a Coke* campaign now lets American buyers print their name – or a slogan, like *Amy's 50th birthday* – on an 8-ounce Coke bottle for $5 apiece. (In Australia, due to the much smaller size of our market, the advertising agency, Ogilvy, was limited to printing 150 popular names and slogans on local cans and bottles). This personalised campaign is credited with growing Coke's sales figures for the first time in 10 years, in a contracting market for soft drinks.

- Retailing for just under AUD$15 apiece, personalised jars of Nutella were a hit in Christmas 2015, with the Melbourne Myer store selling 400,000 units, according to

Media Marketing. This was a clever way of capitalising on the Nutella craze that had just exploded that year, where Nutella donuts were being sold daily by the thousands by bakeries and cafes across the state of Victoria.

What is your gift to the world?

We all want to be known for our intelligence and good judgement. And the more senior and successful someone becomes, and the older they get, the more you're likely to hear them talking about their desire to leave a **legacy**.

A legacy is something that someone has achieved and that continues to exist after they stop working or pass away. In a professional context, a legacy is an artifact of the significance of our work and influence; something that survives long after we have moved on to other things.

Our legacy signifies that we were here, and that the work we did matters.

Within a week of starting to write this book, a number of big stars in the entertainment industry passed away, including David Bowie, Natalie Cole, Glenn Frey (The Eagles), Lemmy Kilmister (lead singer for Motorhead), and actor Alan Rickman.

Aged between 67 and 70, most were younger than the average mortality age, and they have each been mourned and celebrated for the value they gave us while they were alive, as well as the enormous and impressive body of work they left behind.

All are artists who will be remembered for their legacy.

Although David Bowie was arguably the most famous of this group, it's Glenn Frey and Lemmy Kilmister who had the biggest impact on me personally.

As one of the lead vocalists for the Eagles, Glenn Frey's voice can be heard on songs from my childhood like *Take It Easy*, *Peaceful Easy Feeling*, *Already Gone*, *Lyin' Eyes*, *New Kid in Town* and *Heartache Tonight*. Frey also had a successful solo career in the 1980s, and his songs were featured in cult classics of my youth including *Beverley Hills Cop*, *Miami Vice* and *Thelma & Louise*.

As an adult, I was lucky enough to see the Eagles in concert in their Farewell I and Farewell II tours. Apart from Michael Jackson, they were the most talented and inspiring musicians I've ever had the privilege to see performing live.

As a huge fan of the 1980s comedy series The Young Ones, I'll never forget Lemmy Kilmister belting out *Ace of Spades* as Rik, Neil, Vyvyan and Mike ran for the train to Manchester to represent, with hilarious incompetence, their university Scumbag College on the show *University Challenge*.

Legacy is tangible and memorable, and has an impact much broader than just the people we work with in our immediate team. It is legacy, more than anything else, that defines the true and lasting value of what we do and that shapes us, and the people we choose to work with.

If you're in the business of building things, whether it's bridges, buildings or advertising, you're lucky enough to be creating tangible artifacts every day to define your legacy.

I doubt that many people will remember in detail the speeches and workshops I gave, or the new business pursuits I worked on (other than a few of the really big ones). But I hope that many more might remember my books, if they have been inspired or helped by them in some way.

In the context of creating commercial value, identifying the legacy a customer wants to achieve and leading the efforts to co-create that legacy has enormous power.

Here are some questions to ask yourself that identify how what you do helps the customer to do things 'better':

- How does this help the client do things better than their competitors?

- Does this offer innovation or new ideas compared to other methods?

- How will it make the client look smart, for example by bringing in cutting-edge technologies or ideas?

- How does this connect the dots or arrange existing information in a fresh, insightful way?

- How does it fit with the client's desire to make a mark or leave a legacy?

- Will this have a measurable impact on other goals or initiatives without extra cost?

- Are there sustainable benefits that persist after the work is completed?

- Will this enhance the client's reputation, offer kudos or positive media attention?

I hope that this chapter has sparked some ideas about how you can help your customers to do things Better and Smarter.

Combine these with the visceral attributes Cheaper and Safer, and the logical attributes Faster and Simpler, and you've got a formula for new business success.

So this is where I must leave you – at least for now.

But as I said when we started this journey together, this book is just the beginning.

Please reach out to me if you'd like help exploring and applying the concepts we have talked about here.

I'd love to help you win the business you want, at the margins you want, and have more fun while you're doing it.

Where to from here

ROBYN HAYDON IS ONE of Australia's leading experts on business development, helping organisations to build value that supports new business acquisition and customer retention. She is also a specialist in business that is won through formal, competitive bids and tenders.

Robyn is on a mission to break down artificial barriers that keep buyers and sellers from creating value together, and in the process to bring cooperation, energy, and enthusiasm back to the field of business development.

Through her work, Robyn hopes to build a legacy of strong, capable businesses and individuals who see it as a privilege to win and serve customers, and who are empowered to bring the best of themselves to their business development role – no matter what their 'other' roles may be.

- Book Robyn to speak at your next sales meeting, strategy retreat or conference

- Engage Robyn to help you and your team build value-based offers that win new business pursuits

- Talk to Robyn about organisational training and capacity building programs in commercial value creation, tender and proposal leadership, and customer and contract retention

- Check out Robyn's public training programs, including

    ◊ From Chance to Choice: how to make smarter decisions to bid,

    ◊ Persuasive Tender and Proposal Writing Program,

    ◊ Persuasive Speed Writing, and

    ◊ How To Retain Your Most Important Contracts and Customers

- Purchaser Robyn's other books *The Shredder Test – a step-by-step guide to writing winning proposals* and *Winning Again – a retention game plan for your most important contracts and customers*

- Subscribe to Robyn's weekly newsletter, The Winning Pitch

- Connect on LinkedIn or get in touch directly

www.robynhaydon.com
robyn@robynhaydon.com

+61 (0)3 9557 4585

Connect on LinkedIn: https://au.linkedin.com/in/robynhaydon